Washington's Savior

General John Glover
and the
American Revolution

Richard A. Brayall

HERITAGE BOOKS
2013

HERITAGE BOOKS
AN IMPRINT OF HERITAGE BOOKS, INC.

Books, CDs, and more—Worldwide

For our listing of thousands of titles see our website
at
www.HeritageBooks.com

Published 2013 by
HERITAGE BOOKS, INC.
Publishing Division
5810 Ruatan Street
Berwyn Heights, Md. 20740

Copyright © 2013 Richard A. Brayall

Other Heritage Books by the author:

"To the Uttermost of My Power":
The Life and Times of Sir William Pepperrell, 1696–1759

A Note on the Type: This book was set by Microsoft Word for Windows 7 in 12-point and 10-point Bookman Old Style.
The font was designed in 1860 by Alexander Phemister as a serif alternative to the Colon typeface. Bookman Old Style body and headline type is used in publications and it functions well in advertising. The font design was updated twice in the 20th Century.

International Standard Book Numbers
Paperbound: 978-0-7884-5406-6
Clothbound: 978-0-7884-9325-6

Contents

Washington's Savior

Acknowledgements

The writing of any book is a major project where the author often is physically at home but mentally far, far away trying to create or explain his or her idea or vision.

I am no exception.

Because of that, I thank my wife Danita for her patience, understanding and criticism – in no particular order – during the year it took to research and write the manuscript that eventually morphed into this book. She and my three grown sons – Aaron, Trevor and Spencer – also served as my sounding boards for ideas as the work progressed.

Thanks to my son Trevor who took all of the original photographs in this work. This is his second such project for me.

Thanks also to my son Aaron and my mother-in-law Mrs. Antonio Cercone, Jr., both of whom bravely volunteered a second time to proofread one of my manuscripts.

More thanks for research goes to the Massachusetts Historical Society in Boston and in particular to the incomparable Elaine Grublin.

Also, continued thanks for publishing to Leslie Wolfinger of Heritage Books. And thanks to a long list of publishers who allowed me to quote from a number of works they brought to print.

Dedication

After much thought, I decided to dedicate this book to my maternal grandfather, who died 40 years ago. He was a proud graduate of eighth grade and he would have enjoyed John Glover. He died in March of my senior year in high school. These vivid memories show something about the man.

Woodrow Wilson got his first vote, but Harry Truman was his favorite president.

His favorite television character was Ralph Kramden, then Fred Flintstone.

He would call his best friend – his brother – George every Friday evening. That was the only night he stayed up past 7 P.M.

He was a great Red Sox fan who recalled 1918 – I only wish he could have been here for 2004.

His first new car was a doozey – a 1955 Chevrolet.

He retired in 1960 when he was proud to be making $100 per week.

He served in the Navy during World War I aboard the *USS Reina Mercedes*, a gunboat captured from Spain in 1898. It served as a station ship at the Naval Academy and the best thing about it was, he told me, that it had no engine.

Thank you, Gramp.

Washington's Savior

This book is for my Grandfather,
Harry Thomas Whenal
1895 to 1969

John Glover of Massachusetts

Washington's Savior

Preface

John Who?

I first "met" John Glover about nine years ago when I watched the A&E Network's dramatic production of Howard Fast's book *The Crossing*.

A factual look at the Battle of Trenton, the program starred Sebastian Roche as Colonel John Glover, and Jeff Daniels as George Washington. Daniels' portrayal of Washington was a typical character study of the distant, almost god-like personality that the Virginia planter has acquired over the years

Roche's Glover was the stereotypical, bigoted, opinionated, and self-righteous Massachusetts man – not unlike many New Englanders then and today.

Fast and the producers pulled no punches, at one point having a frustrated Washington blurts out to him – "Glover, you are a hard man to like!" How true. And I am sure he would not have wanted it any other way. John Glover was one of a number of soldiers, legislators, administrators and diplomats who worked hard, sacrificed their health and well-being and risked their lives for the American Revolution. Some were remembered, others forgotten, and most were consigned to rattle around in local memories and local libraries.

John Glover was neither present at the creation, nor in uniform at the surprising end of the American Revolution. He surely was not a founding father. He was, however, one thing the army always needed – a soldier of the Revolution.

If Washington was the indispensable man for the Revolution, then people like Glover became equally so, for the good general.

In 1775, John Glover was the colonel of a militia regiment from Marblehead, Massachusetts. Every man was a well-trained soldier, but they also possessed extra skills because every man was also well versed in handling small boats in difficult waters.

Glover and his men saved Washington and the Revolution with their boats, oars and strong arms in the waters of New York; those same men allowed the army to mature on the banks of the Delaware; some brought it to full flower on the banks of the Hudson at Saratoga.

John Glover is no stranger to those familiar with the literature of the Revolution. He is frequently cited but rarely explained in volumes large and small. And he is almost always linked with the fights at Brooklyn or Trenton. But he did much more.

Key to Glover was his relationship to

Washington's Savior

George Washington. In the conclusion of his book, Howard Fast says there were vast differences between the two men that would forever preclude them from having a close friendship.

Washington was of the Virginian planter class, Glover was from the Massachusetts 'mechanic' strata, and that was a wide chasm to cross. Washington was an Episcopalian; Glover was a Congregationalist, and that was often a volatile mixture. Washington was a slave owner and was a reluctant proponent of the 'peculiar institution.'

John Glover's story is one of relationships, relationships with his family, his soldiers, George Washington, and with his own destiny. Today much of the story is about memory, people and places. And things. After all, when all things are said and done what is left to us but memory? It is the one thing that keeps us in touch with the past and that can help all of us prepare for the future. Memory defines each individual throughout their time on earth. But without rekindling, memory often fades away.

Who today remembers Otho Williams?[1]

---

[1] Williams eventually became a general in the Maryland Line; Smallwood was also a Maryland major general. John Haslet was called the best soldier in the Delaware Line until his death at Princeton on January 3, 1777. Mifflin fought much of the war in the Pennsylvania line. Warner and Stark were long-serving colonels in the New Hampshire militia, both of whom played major roles in the Battle of Bennington, Vermont, in 1777, as part of the Saratoga campaign. Both men distrusted Washington and the

Washington's Savior

William Smallwood? John Haslet? Thomas Mifflin? Seth Warner? John Glover? Let's rekindle John Glover.

RAB

Sandown, NH
April 24, 2009

Continental Army and refused commissions from the General. John Glover is the subject of this book.

BOOK ONE

<u>*MASSACHUSETTS* - 1775</u>

The cradle of liberty, the birthplace of independence, the hub of the universe, Taxachusetts – call it what you will, but without Boston, and without the general turmoil and strife that erupted in that colony, there would have been no United States.

Washington's Savior

<u>Chapter 1</u>

A Satisfied Man

General William Howe could not even remember when he had felt more satisfied militarily.[2]

Everything had been planned to the finest detail, and so far all those details had been executed flawlessly by the troops under his command. He smiled when he wondered how much time he would have to plan the surrender of these colonial troops when this accursed war would be over. He expected the surrender would come within days.

The British general – in command of the largest force to ever leave Great Britain – was waiting for the sun to rise and burn off this dreadful fog. When it did, he was sure, this revolution by the American colonies would be over.

Howe's mind raced for a bit, trying to think of the right word to describe this feeling he had in a letter to army headquarters. Satisfied – yes, that would be the right word. He was very satisfied. He would be even more satisfied when

---

[2] This chapter was compiled from a number of sources, but not all of it can be confirmed. It is in essence historical fiction.

Mrs. Loring[3] would join him on Manhattan Island. That is when everything would be on an even keel.

The American rebellion had been a difficult[4] assignment for General William Howe and his brother Richard, who, as an admiral, commanded the ships in which Howe's army had traveled from England to Boston to Halifax and then on to New York. It was, Howe reminded himself, the largest armed force the British had ever sent to fight overseas. It was his responsibility to insure the sanctity of the army and make sure it remained intact and inviolate. But it still must be victorious.

Oh, there had been rewards. Howe himself was very proud that he had been knighted for his work in Boston in 1775. Now he was very pleased to be called Sir William, and he would be Viscount Howe when his elder brother the Admiral passes on.

There were political problems with this assignment. In addition to being a general, Howe was also a Member of Parliament, a minority

---

[3] The beautiful, voluptuous Mrs. Joshua Loring was General Howe's current mistress. They first met in Boston during the siege, and Howe made her husband commissioner, which kept him very busy. Both Lorings were happy with the situation, which was very profitable for them all.

[4] Admiral Richard "Black Dick" Howe currently held the family title of Viscount or Lord Howe. An older brother, George Augustus, had been killed while attacking Fort Ticonderoga during the last of the French wars.

member who belonged to the Whig Party[5] which officially opposed the government. It put Howe in the position of doing all he could to benefit his political enemies.

Difficulties and More Difficulties

Howe knew that he would be very generous with terms once Washington realized that he was defeated and finally surrendered.

But difficulties had still predominated so far in 1776, Howe remembered. It had been difficult ever since he had arrived in Boston with Generals Burgoyne and Clinton, and met with General Gage to discuss the situation. And the situation was damn bad.

Ever since the fighting at Lexington and Concord in April of 1775, the colonials and their militia had surrounded the town of Boston and cut the people from their normal source of provisions and food from outside of the town. Then in June, the debacle took place at Breed's Hill, where he had to watch his troops march into the teeth of the rebel lines and simply die. Yes, they finally broke those damn rebel lines after three charges and the death of a thousand men, but they could not break the rebels. In fact, the General remembered, how the rebels seemed to

---

[5] The British political system at that time consisted of two organizations – the Tories and Whigs. Tories evolved into today's Conservative Party. Whigs became the 20th Century's Liberal Party, which was supplanted in the 1930's by the Labour Party.

get stronger and more determined in the winter, and especially after that so-called General Washington arrived. He seemed to put some iron into those militia groups; groups Howe felt his army could slice through like cheese. Now he wasn't quite so sure.

Then Howe frowned a bit when he remembered the morning in March when he woke up and found heavy artillery embedded in the rebel lines on Dorchester Heights overlooking Boston.

Without one shot being fired, Washington used those guns from Fort Ticonderoga to force Howe to leave Boston, to board ships with all of his troops and any other citizens who wanted or needed to leave the colonial town.

But now he had Washington right where he wanted him. In this dense, thick and unearthly fog produced by the East River that separated Washington and much of his army from safety, Howe was sure Washington was trapped between the river and Howe's army.

The foolish amateur had paid no attention to his flanks during the recent battle and was flabbergasted when Howe appeared to flank the rebel battle line. How those rebels ran and ran once they saw the saw the British bayonet.

Envisioning Each Other

Howe tried to recall if he had ever met Washington during the Seven Years War, but he didn't think they served together. He knew Washington had fought with Braddock's army against the French at Fort Duquesne, the site of present-day Pittsburgh. But he didn't think the Virginian had served anywhere in the north during that war against the French and their Indian allies.

Howe's service in that conflict took him to Cape Breton Island, which the British put under siege. British soldiers were frustrated by this campaign because the fortress had been taken from the French in 1745. In that year, William Pepperrell, the soldier/merchant from Kittery, Maine, led 4,500 New Englanders against the strongest fortress in the Americas, which they reduced to surrender in just 49 days.

As a reward for his victory, Pepperrell was the first colonial to be honored as a baronet, and he was known hereafter as Sir William.[6]

In spite of that success, however, the great stone fortress of Louisbourg was returned to the French by the peace treaty that concluded the War of the Austrian Succession, which was known in the American colonies as King George's War.

After the second victory at Louisbourg in 1758, Howe helped General James Wolfe capture Quebec and he was at Montreal when General Jeffrey Amherst accepted the surrender of the capital of New France, ending that colonial empire forever.

No, Howe certainly didn't remember Washington at any of those major battles. But it didn't matter anyway, he thought, Washington's

---

[6] Brayall, Richard. *To the Uttermost of my Power*, 2008.

military career would be over as soon as the sun rose. The entire rebel army – they called it the Continental Army – was encamped right in front of him, with its back to the East River, and his brother's navy patrolling the river. All we have to do is fix bayonets and we will see these so-called soldiers run.

They ran yesterday, they will run tomorrow. But they won't have far to run – the river will stop them.

Howe now saw the sunlight breaking through the dark skies and he knew his skirmishers would soon be making contact with the rebels as they probed the enemy lines. He listened for gunfire but heard nothing.

Then he heard voices outside his tent, men shouting at each other, shouting words Howe couldn't believe. Then his adjutant appeared in the tent and spoke the last words Howe ever believed he would hear on this matter. "My Lord, the enemy is gone."

An unbelieving Sir William left his tent and rode his horse to the American lines. He stopped and stared – they were gone. Some fires still smoked in the fog, and a few tents still were erected to give an appearance of a camp, should the British take a look.

Howe and his staff stopped and stared, the general realizing that Washington had taken EVERYTHING. And everything meant all cannon, all powder, all stores and provisions, all muskets, all shot, and all of the army. Every single soldier Washington had gotten completely away and now he was ready to fight another day.

Washington's Savior

Several of his staff rode to the river's edge and peered out into the rapidly dispersing fog. His soldiers had captured one boat as it tried to leave the bank.   Three men, who, his men told him, were trying to loot the empty campsite, had manned it.   Howe ordered the captives to the prison hulks moored in New York harbor.

The General looked out into the fog and he swore he could see the stern of several full boats entering the fog and safety.

In the Bosom of Safety

About a half mile away, on the Manhattan shore of the East River, a group of men in blue and buff uniforms watched as the last few boats rowed ashore and were quickly unloaded.   The soldiers readily identified most of the officers. There was General Washington in the middle, surrounded by his staff and a few of his key line officers, including General Nathanael Greene, Colonel Henry Knox, General Charles Lee, and General Horatio Gates.

Washington had been one of the last to leave the old camp in Brooklyn. He had fretted all night long over the escape effort and he was very relieved that the work was done and done right.

At the same time, a man of a slight build, about 5 feet 6 inches tall, with curly hair under his tricorn hat, walked by those last boats to come ashore making certain that everything was secure and stowed away properly. He walked with the command of a man who knew his job and did it properly.

Washington's Savior

The slight man was Colonel John Glover, the commander of the 14th Continental Regiment. That unit of the George Washington's Army was actually a militia regiment made up mostly of boatmen and fishermen who worked on the water for a living. During the previous night they rowed the entire army to safety.

Glover walked over to Washington and the others, and saluted the commander. "Sir," he said. "It is done. The army is all here."

The Virginian nodded. "Thank you, Colonel. Tell your men they saved the army, you have our eternal gratitude."

Chapter 2

Family Origins

Roger Conant and his men were looking for a home in 1626. They were all veteran fishermen who prowled the ocean waters off the coast of New England for the past several years, looking for bountiful catches of fish.

Right now, they lived in a bleak village on the coast of Cape Ann in the Massachusetts Colony, just to the north of where they were right now. Where they were now was at the mouth of the Naumkeag River, with a wooded shoreline that could provide safe haven for his men and their families during the freezing New England winters and the equally hot summer months. They called the settlement Salem, a shortened form of Jerusalem that also was derived from the Hebrew word "shalom," meaning greetings.

The settlement was incorporated in 1629, and shortly thereafter, John Endicott supplanted Roger Conant as governor, by the authority of the Massachusetts Bay colonial government in Boston. Salem grew rapidly as more and more immigrants came to the New England shore to seek fame, fortune or property. It became a shipping and trading center that saw it rival, but never surpass, Boston.[7]

---

[7] Founded in 1630, the town of Boston was established by the Puritans, not the Pilgrims. It is located on the Shawmut

A Dark Place of Foreboding

Salem's darkest moment came in 1692 when a series of church-sponsored trials resulted in the execution of a number of local residents on the charge of witchcraft. For weeks, charges and counter-charges of witchcraft and satanic worship terrorized the citizens while equally ignorant and bigoted judges and ministers did not help the situation. Then, just as suddenly as it had popped up, the witch scare faded away. But psychological scars remained with the town and its inhabitants for years after the memories of the witch trials faded into legend.

William Phipps of Maine was appointed governor of the entire Massachusetts Bay Colony and vowed such horrors would never be revisited on the residents again.

As Salem's population grew, various sections of the original land grant were split off to become a number of other Massachusetts communities. Once the town contained most of the famous "north shore" suburbs of Boston, Salem gave birth to the communities of Peabody, Middleton, Manchester-by-the-Sea, Topsfield, and Wenham.

Salem Village, the section of the town

Peninsula, and in those days it was linked to the mainland by a narrow strip of land known as Boston Neck. The original name of the town was Trimountaine; it was renamed Boston, after a town in Lincolnshire, England. Although it was the capital of Massachusetts from the start, Boston did not become a city until 1832.

linked to the witch trials, became the town of Danvers; in 1649, the last subdivision created the town of Marblehead.

The Glovers Arrive

In this community, residents found their livelihood came from two elements that impacted their lives daily – the land and sea through farming, fishing and trading. Town records indicate that in 1630 a Charles Glover emigrated from England to settle in Salem; by 1640, he had become a member of the First Church. In 1660, his son, John, took a bride, Mary Guppy of Salem, and settled down to raise a family.

One of their sons was named Jonathan. Born in 1677, he married Abigail Henderson on the last day of March in 1697. Their eldest son, also named Jonathan, married Tabitha Bacon on February 23rd, 1727. Jonathan Jr. was the father of John Glover from the Marblehead regiment that fought in the Revolution, (my John Glover) and his three brothers - Jonathan, Samuel and Daniel. John was the third-born, arriving in this world on November 5th, 1732. He was baptized at Salem's First Church.

Tragedy struck the family, however, when John's father died when the younger Glover was only four years old. Tabitha now took over the family and she decided to leave Salem Village and move to Marblehead. In this new community, she was able to send all of her children to school, where they all learned how to read and write.

Then her boys all undertook the responsibility to learn a trade to support the family and become a respectable part of the community.

To that end, the Glover boys each apprenticed to a local artisan in order to learn a profitable trade. Samuel became a goldsmith, John a shoemaker, and Daniel was a block maker. These were not, however, exciting or glamorous professions. One by one, the Glover boys sought out and found new occupations. And with Marblehead right on the Atlantic Ocean and a key part of the fishing industry, its position encouraged hearty residents to consider sea-faring jobs.

John Glover was eager to answer the call of the sea. He worked hard on several fishing boats plying their trade on the fishing banks off the Atlantic coast; within a few years, Glover was able to purchase his own fishing schooner. That allowed him to make more profit, and to invest more in his business, and to expand the scope and variety of his operations.

He found excellent markets for goods and products across the Atlantic in Spain and Portugal, and he and his brothers worked the trade routes diligently. He was becoming a member of "the cod fish aristocracy" that ruled Massachusetts, "the land of the bean and the cod."

The brothers used their business acumen to build up their personal fortunes as well as to construct large two-story homes on the main street of their hometown as well as well as substantial buildings that held their business operations.

In the meantime, warfare had come to the colonies again in 1757 as the French and their Indian allies tried to push the British into the sea. Samuel Glover went off to war that year and served as a captain in several colonial militia regiments until the end of the war. As a soldier, Samuel Glover witnessed the fall of Quebec and Montreal and the complete domination of New France by the British

Soon Glover ships were returning from Spain, Portugal and the Caribbean with goods that would be sold profitably in Marblehead and other communities.

Contemporary reports indicated that Glover was a shrewd businessman who could drive a hard bargain with the toughest of customers. He was most likely a frugal, austere, and flinty individual like many other New Englanders.

A Commercial Leader

By the beginnings of the revolutionary strife in 1770, Glover was a leading figure in the town's merchant hierarchy. Eventually, he owned and managed his own fleet, featuring the ship *Hannah*, which would play a prominent role in Glover's future.

In addition to building a thriving business, Glover also was busy building a strong and thriving family. On November 30th, 1754, John

Glover married Hannah Gale, also of Marblehead. Together, they had eleven children,

They were:

John, **Jr.**, born 1756, served with his father; Later lost at sea;
Hannah, 1756, died in infancy;
Daniel, 1759, died in infancy;
Hannah, 1761;
Samuel, 1762;
Jonas, 1764;
Tabitha, 1765;
Susannah, 1765;
Sarah, 1773;
Mary, 1769; and
Jonathan, 1774.

A Tradition of Arms

Since its inception, Marblehead had encouraged and maintained a distinctive tradition of militia service. Although the town was located on the Atlantic coast and seemed far removed from typical inland communities that often were subjected to attack from the French and Indians, Marblehead was proud of its town defense force.

People in Marblehead were not about to shirk their duties to protect their friends, families, and fellow citizens. The result was the second largest standing militia in the colony – more than 1,000 men ready to fight at a moment's notice.

A consistent thread running through the

ranks of the militia was the presence of a Glover in the leadership roles, especially John Glover. Records show that on March 12th, 1759, he was commissioned an ensign in the Third Military Foot Company of the Marblehead Militia. Massachusetts Royal Governor Thomas Pownall signed the formal commission document.

A second commission for Glover, signed by Governor Francis Bernard on February 12th, 1762, noted his election to the rank of captain lieutenant in the Marblehead militia. A third commission signed by Governor Thomas Hutchinson in 1773 indicated that Glover was now a captain of foot infantry in the Marblehead militia, serving under Colonel John Gallinson, and then Colonel Jeremiah Lee.

In addition to their work in the fishing industry and the militia, the Glovers devoted additional efforts at improving their hometown by serving in a variety town government posts, such as selectman and town meeting moderator. Through mostly time-consuming and tedious roles, the Glovers nonetheless showed their commitment to public service.

The Inoculation Wars

In the early 1770's, their devotion to the health and well being of their community and citizens almost caused bloodshed among them in the unusual undertaking.

Apparently the Glover brothers were modern thinkers when it came to some updated medical practices. They especially advocated the use of inoculations to stop the spread of small pox as the disease made regular inroads in the American colonies.

In fact, during the early 1770's, the brothers opened a special hospital on Cat Island in Salem Harbor. This hospital specialized in small pox inoculation and was controversial from the very start.

Both Glovers were determined not to give in to ignorant public opinion and compromise their own personal beliefs. Jonathan Glover was so adamant to stand his ground that legend says he actually had loaded cannon in his front hall, aimed at the front door of his home, just in case the other side tried to solve the stand-off with violence.

The "inoculation" wars did split the community however. By 1774, the majority of citizens were opposed to the hospital and it was closed by a vote at the annual town meeting. That decision could have been a major problem for the town, because it caused the two Glovers and many of their friends, like Azore Orne and Elbridge Gerry, to withdraw from local politics and leave those problems to the opposition. But that all changed when rumor of war and fighting against the British came to them from the north, from the colony called New Hampshire.

Washington's Savior

Chapter 3

The First Shots

The strife that now afflicted the American colonies actually begun when Parliament felt little stamps could pay for big wars and passed the Stamp Act of 1765.

They also thought free Englishmen in America would happily reimburse the Mother Country for finally driving off the French. They were wrong on both counts. Although the fighting at Lexington and Concord is normally cited as the seminal moment of the American Revolution, conflict had also begun in different places before that "April morn" in Middlesex County, Massachusetts.

In December 1774, news came to Marblehead about gunfire and rebellion in the north, some 50 miles away in another colony – New Hampshire.

On the 14th of that month, citizens in Portsmouth, the capital of the province, and under the leadership of patriot John Langdon, stormed and quickly overwhelmed the small British garrison at Fort William and Mary in Newcastle. This stone fort guarded the entrance to the mouth of the Piscataqua River and it was one of the oldest defensive positions in the colonies[8]. So when they left it, they left the gates open so the British could come back. But they returned only after Langdon and his men divided a large store of munitions kept there into smaller packets and sent them on to outlying towns beyond the reach of the British.

News of the Portsmouth insurgency spread rapidly throughout New England and it interested Jonathon and John Glover. They knew the King had fewer resources in New Hampshire than he had in Massachusetts. Such an attack against any fortified British position here would be much more difficult to pull off than it had been to the north.

A Watchful Interregnum

For several years now, people throughout British America had cringed as London tried to impose special taxes on the American colonies to help retire the large debt England had incurred in fighting the French and Indian War from 1754 to 1760. England started with the Stamp Act, which prompted riots and disturbances throughout the colonies until it was repealed in the mid-1760s. In fact, all the tax attempts over the years were repealed except for the tax on tea. And that tax ultimately prompted the infamous "Boston Tea Party" in the cold of December 1773.

Boston, which felt it was also victimized by the "Massacre" of 1770, was ordered to pay for all

---

[8] This old bulwark of stone on the south shore of the Piscataqua was eventually taken into formal possession by the Patriots and was renamed Fort Constitution.

the tea dumped in the harbor and Boston refused. As a result of this refusal, the London government began to pass a series of laws – collectively known as the Intolerable Acts – designed to punish the town and its citizens; to turn the town into a shadow of its former self; and to make sure it never again rose to economic prominence.

The Intolerable Acts

For some time as the Boston drama unfolded, the twelve other colonies in British North America closely watched the situation in Boston as the British Parliament continued to pass act after act aimed at punishing the colonial port of Boston and the entire colony of Massachusetts.

The worst of the Intolerable Acts – the Boston Port Act – closed the port of Boston to all commercial shipping from any country except England. In the end, the British soldiers in Boston eagerly and tightly applied this legislation. The townspeople began to really hate and distrust the "lobster backs," as they called the British.

Only British ships could enter the port, which was becoming a ghost harbor. The Intolerable Acts also levied a severe fine on the town that had to be paid by the citizens; imposed martial law; removed Governor Thomas Hutchinson and installed General Thomas Gage in his place; billeted thousands of soldiers, essentially dissolving the General Court and the Governors Council – the colonial legislature.

Washington's Savior

Other Massachusetts communities – and the rest of the colonies in British North America – were shocked by the severity of the sanctions. No British colony or community had ever been treated so harshly by its own government.

Many people in the colonies were convinced that this was the work of the evil ministers and not their good King George III.   But eventually everyone found out that just the opposite was true – the King wanted to teach his loyal colonists a lesson once and for all.

The harsh British treatment of Boston aroused substantial sympathy from the other twelve colonial governments.   Some colonies offered aid, such as food and clothing, while others suggested other assistance, such as militia organizations and also munitions, to be sent to the beleaguered town.

Marbleheaders Support Boston Brethren

The good citizens of Marblehead now had the chance to make a nice profit off of the internal problems that swirled around what was, in reality, a major commercial rival.   According to the Port Act, the Custom House – the center of tax and collecting usually by local officials – was to be assigned to Marblehead until further notice. At this point in time, however, Marblehead informed the Crown that the Custom House would not be welcomed in the community.   The town would stand solidly behind Boston and they would not use the Bostonians unfortunate situation for their own benefit or profit.

The Continental Congress

One positive result of the Intolerable Acts took place on September 5, 1774, when the First Continental Congress convened in Philadelphia, then the capital of Pennsylvania and the leading seaport and largest city in the colonies. Composed of more than 50 delegates from all colonies except Georgia, which did not attend, the conference was called to discuss ways to lessen the impact on the Intolerable Acts on Boston and the other colonies. And for many, the convening of the congress was seen as the first step on the road to colonial unity and perhaps eventual independence.

This First Continental Congress was able to accomplish little during its brief lifetime, but it did call for a second congress to gather in Philadelphia in 1775. That meeting would change the world.

One of the more notable victims of the Intolerable Acts was the historic and venerable General Court, the colony's legislature. This group did not dissolve as ordered by the Crown. Instead, it reconvened outside of Boston, called itself the Massachusetts Provincial Congress and claimed for itself de facto legislative power for the colony. The group also laid claim to control the local militia as well as all of the munitions and fortifications in the colony. It also retained its loyalty and fealty to King George.

Meanwhile, all the Glovers were kept busy in Marblehead, busy with the fishing industry, with their hospital, and with training as John worked to polish the militia unit. They found other things to do as well. As dissatisfaction with the British had grown, revolutionary groups like the Sons of Liberty had foreseen the need to communicate with each other and with other organizations. So they set up Committees of Correspondence composed of men who kept in contact with each other and shared ideas. One of those writers in Marblehead was John Glover.

A Friend with a Future

Another writer and committee member was an old friend of Glover's named Elbridge Gerry. They were allies on the hospital issue – they had gone to school together, had matured together, and had worked together. But they served the Revolution in different ways.

Glover went to war. Gerry counted votes and went to the Continental Congress where he became a leader of what eventually became the Democratic Republican party of Thomas Jefferson.

After the war, Gerry served in Congress for several terms and also became Governor of Massachusetts. While serving in that office he became well known for developing convoluted and salamander-like redistricting plans, shaped like the lizard, so that his party would retain seats in Congress. This activity is still undertaken today by state legislatures and is still known as gerrymandering – named after Elbridge Gerry. In 1812, Gerry became Vice President of the United States under James Madison, serving in that office until he died in 1814.

It did not take long before all communities in Massachusetts were now on alert, as a strange waiting game began to evolve throughout the colony. By now, John Glover was the lieutenant colonel of the Marblehead regiment, the second in command.

The Salem Alarm

On February 27th, 1774, a cold Sunday afternoon, residents of Marblehead who happened to look seawards were surprised to see British warships off the coast, lower whaleboats full of soldiers and see those boats make for a landing on a deserted beach at Homan's Cove. Within the hour, 300 men under Colonel Alexander Leslie were in formation and on the march toward Salem. The British colonel had been ordered to make his way to the north shore town and seize a large supply of munitions the townspeople had collected illegally.

Leslie moved his men quickly, but not quite quickly enough. He had problems crossing a drawbridge on the North River, and then had a verbal confrontation with an armed group of Salem patriots. Finally, after hours of talks with the armed residents and militia in Salem, Leslie returned to his ships in the sea off the shore at

Marblehead. He returned to his garrison without bloodshed – and without the munitions.

One thing Colonel Leslie had not seen anywhere during the day was the militia of Marblehead. As the column approached the beach after dark, however, Leslie could see why. Standing in front of them was Glover's militia, waiting, watching and protecting their town. Leslie and his men had to pass through the ranks of the militia to reach the sea.

Glover's men were not "minutemen," they were not able to instantly be in formation. But they had been gathered quickly from church, the field, the sea, or wherever they were. Then they waited.

Glover and his men watched until Leslie and his redcoats were safely aboard their ships.

The Salem Alarm, as Leslie's incursion was called, was yet another warning for colonials that their perceived rights and personal liberties were in jeopardy. General Gage and his men were equally determined to enforce the King's edicts and laws in dealing with the port of Boston and the colonials in Massachusetts. A deadly clash was inevitable.

It came on April 19th, 1775.

Lt. Colonel Francis Smith was given an assignment similar to Colonel Leslie's. Smith's task was to seize munitions and hopefully capture rebel leaders John Hancock and Samuel Adams and took him west to the villages of Lexington and Concord.

In the early light of the spring morning, Lt.

Washington's Savior

Jesse Adair led a column of redcoats into Lexington, where the town militia had been waiting all night for courage, to hold steady and that "If they mean to have a war, let it begin here."

It did.

The two forces stared each other down, then a single soldier – no one to this day knows if the man was a Redcoat or a Patriot – suddenly flinched and fired. Then the normal quiet of the early morning hours of Middlesex County was broken by the volleys of muskets as both sides tried to maintain order in their lines. Slowly, Adair had his men disengage and begin their to march to reunite with Smith on Concord road. By the time the British left the town, the Lexington Green was littered with the bodies of seventeen Patriots, the first Americans to pay the ultimate price, in what would become a very long war for freedom and independence.

Things Could Never be the Same Again

Lt. Colonel Smith reunited with Adair and continued on to Concord where his men fought the patriots at the famous Concord Bridge. By the time the column met a relief force sent from Boston, they were exhausted and surrounded by militiamen from a variety of communities west of Boston. The militia fired at the Redcoats from behind trees and stonewalls with deadly accuracy. By the time they had marched the sixteen miles to Boston, they had lost several hundred men.

Washington's Savior

The local militia meanwhile, had totally invested Boston. The royal capital of the crown colony of Massachusetts was now under siege by its own citizens. It was a world turned upside down.

In addition, alarms rang throughout the four New England colonies and the people responded. Citizen soldiers and militia units from all four colonies made their way to Boston.

The Massachusetts Provincial Congress, the rump of the dissolved colonial General Court, took what control any one could extract from the situation. One thing it did do was to adopt all the militia units around Boston into a quasi-army under the control of the colony and not the Crown. It also named Artemis Ward to head the Army. A little over 75 years old, Ward was a veteran of the French and Indian War and probably one of the few men qualified for command of such forces. In addition to his military experience, Ward had also served as the top officer of the colonial militia for the colony.

The men of Marblehead heard about the fighting to the west and the militia assembled and quickly determined the force of 20,000 troops surrounding Boston was sufficient for now. Instead of marching on the capital and adding to the confusion there, they decided the Marblehead regiment would stay and guard the north shore from any further British incursion either by sea or from the north in New Hampshire.

Lexington and Concord had a very direct impact on John Glover. On April 17th, John Hancock and Sam Adams were on their way there to meet with some men from Marblehead. Elbridge Gerry, Azor Orne[9] and Colonel Jeremiah Lee spent most of the day with Hancock and Adams to discuss the munitions situation for the town and their future.

By the end of the day, the spring weather turned cold and rainy as Hancock and Adams moved to the west towards Lexington and Concord. The Marblehead men also had to travel some distance in this inclement weather, and by the time they got home, Colonel Lee was stricken with a severe cold. This normally mild affliction weakened Lee and he died three weeks later.

His passing left a vacancy at the top of the regiment, and John Glover, as the lieutenant colonel, was his natural successor. When the regiment voted, it elected him unanimously to the colonelcy; the men never regretted their choice.

Glover also knew one thing could save many of his men during battle and that was discipline. He began to drill them daily and it was not long before his regiment evolved into a well-oiled, well-drilled, and well-commanded unit.

Nearly two weeks later, the Massachusetts militia was absorbed by the Continental Army

---

[9] Azore Orne was a member of a prominent Marblehead family and a lifelong friend of John Glover. Of the three great Marbleheaders during the Revolution, Glover went to war, Elbridge Gerry went to Congress, and Azore Orne stayed home to run the town. Born in 1731, Orne died on June 6th, 1796.

and then given the designation of 21st Regiment. There would be one more change.

The officer's list for the 21st Regiment was;

Colonel - John Glover
Lt. **Colonel** - John Gerry
Major - Gabriel Johonett
Adjutant - William Gibbs
Captains - William R. Lee, William Courtis, William Bacon, Thomas Grant, Joel Smith, Nicholson Broughton, William Blacklet, John Merit, John Selman, Francis Symonds.
Lieutenants - John Glover, Jr., Robert Harris, William Mills, William Bubier, John Bray, John Stacy, Nathaniel Clark, Joshua Prentice, Isaac Collyer, William Russell.
Ensigns - Edward Archbold, Thomas Courtis, Seward Lee, Ebenezer Graves, Joshua Orne, J. Devereax, Jr., Nathaniel Pierce, Robert Nimbblett, Edward Holman, George Lingrass.

A Revolutionary Community

Almost more than any other community in New England, Marblehead quickly and permanently attached itself to the uprising that would become the American Revolution. And it, like many other communities in the region, Marblehead, paid a heavy price for its involvement in the revolution, and economic figures tell the story fairly well. Pre-revolutionary records show that the port handled 12,000 tons of cargo per year; by 1780 that figure had been reduced to just 50 tons.

In addition, almost every family was involved in the conflict either in Glover's regiment or with a variety of privateers sent out by community ship owners. At the end of the Revolution, Marblehead was the home of at least 966 fatherless children, their fathers having died in combat from Massachusetts to South Carolina or having died at sea of either disease or wounds suffered during the many naval battles of the Revolution. No community of equal size in any of the 13 colonies suffered as much as this Massachusetts town.

Preparing for War

Some time in the early 1770's, the Glovers apparently abandoned Marblehead as the site of their commercial operations. Instead, they moved their business operations, including all shipping and docking facilities, to the nearby community of Beverly. Beverly was becoming a commercial rival to Salem, although it would never surpass the "Witch City." The Glovers remained residents of Marblehead.

On May 22nd, the Marblehead Regiment, which had been taking orders from the Massachusetts Provincial Congress, was officially transferred to the control of the Second Continental Congress in Philadelphia, which by default had become the government of the united colonies. Glover and his men awaited orders.

Again, events began to move rapidly.

Washington's Savior

On May 25th, a British warship – *HMS Cerberus*, named after the three-headed dog in Greek mythology that guards the gates of Hell – sailed into Boston Harbor with three major generals – William Howe, John Burgoyne and Henry Clinton.

They were sent by London to advise General Gage how to break the siege of Boston. It certainly seemed as if the British already had enough "brass" in the town to come up with a sensible plan, but instead they decided to follow a scheme devised by General Howe.

The Battle of Bunker Hill

The basics of the plan called for some 4,000 troops to cross Boston Harbor after night fall by small boats and attack the works the colonials recently occupied on a tall hill in Charlestown.

On June 17th, General Howe made his move, although he attacked Breed's Hill, a smaller, closer rise, and not Bunker Hill. In retrospect, it did not matter which hill he attacked because this time the militia didn't run. They waited until they saw the white's of the British eyes, and fired. And fired. And fired.

Howe watched his men march up the hill to slaughter three times before they took the summit and they only took it because the Patriots ran out of ammunition. The carnage was horrendous on both sides, but the British suffered the most. Howe lost close to 1,000 men. The sights on the top of the hill and both slopes were gruesome to the extreme. New Hampshire militia Colonel John Stark later said "the dead lay thicker than sheep in a fold."

Dr. Joseph Warren, the head of the Massachusetts Provincial Congress, told friends he had a premonition he would die in the upcoming battle. He scoffed at his dream and told everyone not to believe such foolishness. After the battle, British soldiers found the body of Dr. Warren, shot several times in the back as the patriots withdrew. He was buried in a common grave.

Thanks to the war-like actions of both sides at Lexington and Concord and then again by the Redcoats at Bunker Hill, a "family quarrel" between a group of colonies and their mother country had become a deadly feud with no reconciliation in sight or even wanted by the leadership on either side.

Chapter 4

Boston Besieged

The 55 men in Philadelphia were not exactly sure what to do. They had been sent to the Second Continental Congress essentially to serve as a conservative debating society to try and find out if there was a way they could patch things up with the mother country.

But things kept happening in one colony – Massachusetts. Starting in 1770, the events rolled along and featured a massacre, a tea party, the Intolerable acts aimed at destroying Boston, Lexington and Concord, and now Bunker Hill.

Conservative delegates to the Congress, like Pennsylvanian John Dickinson, told the other delegates that actions by Massachusetts have made it difficult for the other colonies to remain at peace, and even suggested Massachusetts go it alone rather than endanger the other twelve.

In fact, the Continental Congress even sent to England an "olive branch petition" seeking peace and pardon from King George III. Needless to say, Massachusetts did not vote in favor of this effort and George III ruthlessly rejected the petition anyway.

Now these difficult Massachusetts people wanted the Congress to adopt the militia surrounding Boston as an army, a national army.

Washington's Savior

Debate raged on in Philadelphia.

This problem had no easy solution. There were political problems to work out, like how do we handle England now, and they had to deal with thirteen provincial congresses that all had their own power; not to mention the militants that beset them. It seemed they were now responsible for the armed militia surrounding Boston whether or not they wanted it. Thoughts varied about what they should do? Should they adopt the militia army? Should each colony control their own militia? And the delegates knew whatever they did would upset the Crown.

The skirmishes at Lexington and Concord were one thing, but General Howe had taken the bloody conflict with Massachusetts to a new level with his assault on Bunker/Breeds Hill.

One delegate thought he had the answer. John Adams of Massachusetts knew the congress must take advantage of this situation and take control of the militia now they had the opportunity.

Adams also had strong ideas about who should be in charge of the army. The initial commander, Artemis Ward, was too old and he was from Massachusetts. General Israel Putnam was a veteran of the French War and he was already at Boston, but he was from Connecticut and that was a part of New England. What was needed was a general from one of the larger colonies that would promote colonial unity. And Adams knew just who could fit that bill.

The delegates were aware Colonel George

Washington's Savior

Washington of Virginia was a very rich man and a seasoned veteran of the French and Indian War. Washington was not shy about emphasizing his background and he wore his blue and buff Virginia militia uniform to Congress everyday.

A General in Waiting

On June 15, 1775, John Adams asked for recognition and the entire Congress sat up to pay attention. John Hancock from Massachusetts, a rich merchant who was the current president of the Congress, felt he was qualified for the army job and he believed Adams was about to nominate him for it. The Boston merchant prince with the sprawling signature was speechless when Adams proposed Colonel George Washington. The vote was unanimous.

Washington, who stood six feet, three inches tall, accepted the position with grace and humility. He said he was not worthy of their trust, but he would give his best effort to the defense of his country.

Then he took some time to write to his wife, Martha, to explain to her why he was going to Boston and not home. He wrote that he would be home by Christmas – and he would be – by Christmas, 1783.

Washington would in time prove to be a conservative general in terms of the structure and organization. His model for the Continental Army would be the one he was about to fight. In his mind, two battalions would always create a regiment; two regiments a brigade; and two brigades will be a division. He had a great respect for the British Army going back to the days of the French and Indian War. In fact, during the years after the French War, Washington actively and unsuccessfully sought a commission in the regular British army.

The Congress gave Washington a stirring send-off, and on June 25th, he rode north to Boston, with Gen. Charles Lee and Gen. Philip Schuyler.[10]

At the same time, John Glover and the men from Marblehead, were on the move. Ever since Bunker Hill, the regiment had been on alert and had even responded to several false alarms that had Redcoats landing near Marblehead.

Since he had taken over the regiment, Glover, who was no martinet, had drilled and drilled his men so they could march in their sleep and march correctly. He was a tough taskmaster, but he knew good training was often a matter of life and death for his men.

Then four days after Bunker Hill, the Massachusetts Provincial Congress ordered Glover and his regiment, now called the 21st Foot,

---

[10] Schuyler was one of the richest men in the colony of New York, a direct descendant of the early Dutch settlers. He owned vast lands in the Mohawk River Valley. He commanded military activities along the Lake Champlain invasion corridor to and from Canada. He served that capacity until just before the 1777 Saratoga campaign when Horatio Gates replaced him. One of his daughters married Alexander Hamilton. Charles Lee was a former British officer who felt he should be commander-in-chief. He would be a constant pain in Washington's backside.

to Cambridge to join the army besieging Boston. They were state militia now, although that status would shortly change.

Sometime, probably shortly after Bunker Hill, John Glover gave up his extensive business operations and devoted his personal financial resources to the revolutionary cause. Much of his fortune went to outfitting his regiment and fitting out several privateers to attack British shipping.

He apparently made financial arrangements for his family's support during his absence, but is probably true that they were not adequate for what would become a war of eight years. No one thought it would last that long.

The Only Logical Choice

Washington was really the most logical choice for commander in chief. He had taken a roundabout route to success, from a lonely childhood controlled by an unbalanced mother to great wealth obtained through his marriage to Martha.

He attended the entire First Continental Congress and never once spoke in public session; during the second Congress, he spoke very little as well. In addition, every day in Philadelphia he wore his Virginia militia uniform without telling people why. Living near poverty after the early death of his father, George was rescued by his half brother Laurence, from whom he inherited Mount Vernon after his brother died.

Washington's Savior

He later married Virginia's wealthiest widow and instantly became the colony's richest citizen on their nuptials. He was elected to the House of Burgesses, Virginia's legislative assembly, due largely to his wealth; he became a leading figure in the colony.

His record of fighting in the French and Indian War was not stellar. He suffered several defeats during that war – in fact, he started it. But overall, the colonies had no strong tradition of military service.

Their most illustrious military figure was the late Sir William Pepperrell from Maine who died in 1759. Fourteen years before, he had led New England's colonial forces against the fortress of Louisbourg in New France in 1745.

The New General Arrives

On July 3rd, 1775 George Washington and his small entourage rode into the largest of the military camps that ringed Boston. This was in Cambridge, across the River Charles from the besieged town.

His quick arrival surprised many of the people who wanted to see him when he arrived. But what he found in the camp was a disgrace. It had little organization, unequal representation, and no sanitation. Washington was disgusted with it, but he made up his mind that he would reorganize and clean it up. And do it quickly.

Washington met with General Ward and took over command of the army at Cambridge. He moved quickly to clean up the camp and improve sanitary conditions. He worked to reorganize the army and develop a command staff that would work with him closely.

Marblehead Arrives

The very next day, John Glover arrived in camp with his men from Marblehead. If George Washington witnessed the arrival of Glover, he certainly would have been pleased. The smartly dressed men from Marblehead marched into the camp in precise military formation and quickly dispersed to build their campsite. Everything was done with precise military spit and polish. It did not go unnoticed.

You couldn't help but notice the distinctive uniforms the men from Marblehead wore. In many ways, they looked more like the crew of a ship rather than an infantry regiment. All enlisted men wore pants made from white duck cloth, white shirts and short blue jackets. They also wore identical black shoes with pewter buckles. Some companies tarred their pants as sailors often did, which provided yet another image so different from the rest of the army.

Colonel John Glover was resplendent in his own uniform, which was similar to the men's. When he finally left New England for New York, he took with him two broadcloth jackets with fur trimming, six pair of white pants; six pair of white knee breeches with matching socks; two spare pair of shoes; and two extra tricorn hats.

Since Glover was normally on horseback, he wore a pair of matched silver pistols, and other equestrian weapons, including a Scottish broadsword.[11]

The Marblehead regiment was mentioned prominently in Washington's orders of the day for the next 24-hour period. It read:

> It is ordered that Colonel Glover's regiment be ready this evening, with all their accoutrements, to support General Manning of the New Hampshire forces, in case the need arise.

> It is also ordered that Colonel Prescott's regiment equip themselves to march this evening and take possession of the woods leading to Lechmere Point. In case of attack, Colonel Glover's regiment is to march immediately to their support.[12]

Colonel Glover and General Washington also had a minor disagreement over accommodations in Cambridge. When Glover first arrived, he was told to choose one of the abandoned Cambridge mansions for his headquarters. He picked a large white home formerly owned by Tory Colonel John Vassal, and that eventually became known as the Longfellow Mansion, when the famous poet, Henry Wadsworth Longfellow, owned it.

Glover's regiment had been in the house for about two weeks, when a member of Washington's staff told the Colonel that the 14th would have to leave the property because the General wanted it for his headquarters. Glover

---

[11] Upham, William, *A Memoir of General John Glover of Marblehead.*, 1863, p. 6.

[12] Sanborn, Nathan, P., *John Glover and His Marblehead Regiment in the Revolutionary* War, 1903, p. 33.

graciously told the staff member that his men would be out shortly and he turned the home over to Washington for the duration of the siege. In reality, the men of the 14th Regiment were much happier with the new location because it is much closer their favorite tavern.

Opinions

During this time Washington also fell victim to another major colonial problem – inter-colonial rivalries.

It was no secret that men from different colonies did not get along. In New England alone, New Hampshire people didn't like those from Massachusetts and vice versa and no one liked Rhode Islanders. It got worse.

New Englanders hated New Yorkers and no one from the North liked anyone from the South and vice versa. These New England militiamen didn't much like taking orders from a Virginian either.

Washington made the mistake of putting some of his feelings on paper. In a letter to his cousin, Lund, who was managing the family estate and plantation, Mount Vernon, during his absence, Washington wrote: "the officers generally speaking of the most a different kind of people ever you saw and they are exceedingly dirty and nasty people."[13]

In spite of his admiration for Glover and his

---

[13] Scheer and Rankin, *Rebels and Redcoats*, p. 123.

14ᵗʰ Massachusetts Continental Regiment, the General had problems with it too. Like many of the New England military organizations, the Marblehead regiment included people of all walks of life in the community and that included a whole raft of minorities such as blacks, Indians and others. That did not sit well with Washington, who like all slave owners, feared nothing more than an armed slave revolt. Eventually, Washington would get his way and have all such minorities excluded from the Continental Army.

Washington was not alone in expressing such opinions. Alexander Graydon, a captain from Pennsylvania, echoed Washington's sentiments. He noted his admiration for the Marbleheaders, but he did add that "in the regiment there are a number of Negroes, which persons unaccustomed to such associations, has a disagreeable, degrading effect."[14]

Some of these negative reports found their way back to Congress and to John Adams in particular. He was not especially happy to hear how the new commander-in-chief and a great many of his soldiers felt about New Englanders and he let the General know that in no uncertain terms. Washington may not have changed his mind, but he kept his opinions to himself from now on.

It wasn't long before the General got a good look at the problem first-hand. In mid–September, most of Glover's regiment were in an open field near Harvard College on a Saturday

---

[14] Fisher, David Hackett, *Washington's Crossing*, p. 22.

afternoon. His men were minding their own business when a group of Virginia riflemen walked by, led by Captain Daniel Morgan.[15] The groups began making fun of each other's uniforms, then the taunting turned serious and full-fledged fighting broke out.

Washington was at a nearby campsite when he heard the ruckus. Witnesses said he turned red when he saw what was going on and rushed over to the fight. He grabbed one soldier in each strong hand and lifted them up off the ground, telling them to fight their enemies, not their friends. Then he dropped both men to the ground and watched as both units vanished.

Two Good Men

In spite of his initial negative feelings toward New Englanders, the General did find two men from the region to depend on throughout the war. The first was a 37-year-old former Quaker from Rhode Island, with no military training and who had somehow been elected general of that colony's militia. George Washington had liked Nathanael Greene from the minute he met him and that fondness never changed throughout the

---

[15] Daniel Morgan was a famous frontiersman from Virginia. In 1775, he went to Québec with Benedict Arnold and was captured during the unsuccessful attack. He later was exchanged in time to take part in the Battle of Saratoga in 1777. Later, Morgan became quite ill and went home to Virginia to recuperate. In 1781, he became second in command to Nathanael Greene in the South, where he soundly defeated the British at the Battle of the Cowpens. He then retired from the Army due to illness.

war. He always advised Washington well, and he served voluntarily as the quartermaster general during the miserable Valley Forge Winter of 1777.

In 1780, Greene was given command of the Southern Department of the army and told to give battle with Lord Cornwallis. That same year, Washington also told Congress that he would want Greene to succeed him as army commander, if a replacement was ever needed.

The second person Washington embraced was a 25-year-old former bookseller from Boston by the name of Henry Knox. Knox initially served as a volunteer guide for Washington when the Virginian first arrived at Cambridge. Although he had no formal military training, Knox had read prodigiously on the subject of artillery and was considered an expert. He soon became invaluable to Washington and the General begin to groom him to replace the current chief of artillery, Colonel Richard Gridley. Gridley was a veteran of Sir William Pepperrell's Louisbourg campaign in 1745 where he was also chief of artillery.

John Glover was another New Englander who Washington would learn to trust, but he would never be as close to the General as the other two, Greene and Knox.

Guns from Ticonderoga

But as 1775 drew to a close, the stalemate at Boston continued and the siege went on with no sure end in sight. The army was getting bored, men and units were melting away, and Washington feared reinforcements might arrive at anytime in Boston harbor.

Henry Knox had turned the General's focus westward now, to the great pine forest and the Adirondack Mountains in New York, and to the shores of Lake Champlain. On the lake's western shore sat what once was called "the key to the continent" – Fort Ticonderoga.

This French-built-fortress was the scene of several battles during the French and Indian War. Earlier in the year, on May 10, a captain of militia from Connecticut, Benedict Arnold, bloodlessly captured the fort with the assistance of Ethan Allen and his Green Mountain Boys.

Knox knew there were guns at Ticonderoga, cannon of all sizes that could drive the British out of Boston. All he needed to do is go and get them. He explained the plan to Washington and his staff, and Henry Knox volunteered to go get them. No one knew how long it would take.

Gage Goes Home In Disgrace

On October 6th, 1775, a solitary British warship sailed into Boston Harbor.   It was the HMS Scarborough and she was there on official business – to bring Lt. General Thomas Gage home in disgrace. Gage had failed to quell the Massachusetts uprising, and he would be given no more chances.   His world had collapsed around him; and it did even, more so in England when he found out that his wife had been a spy in the pay of the patriots.   The ship set sail for London on October 11th, 1775. General William Howe was in command in America now.

Washington's Savior

Washington understood the need for quick action and good luck as he watched Knox go off to Ticonderoga. He needed some of that god luck himself because the 20,000-man army he had inherited in July was melting away in November.

In spite of improved sanitary conditions, disease ran rampant through the Cambridge camp and other locations occupied by the Continental Army, which were breeding grounds for diseases such as smallpox, typhus, typhoid and other pleasantries.

In spite of their best efforts, Washington and his medical staff were hard pressed to keep the Boston camps clean. As the year progressed, Washington's effective fighting force had been reduced from 20,000 to just about 5,000 men.

His men also had yet to be tested. He did not know how the men would respond to enemy fire or to the throw of the British bayonet. In his mind, a way to find out would be to order a frontal assault on the works behind Boston neck.

What he feared most was a stroke by General Howe that would break the American lines and end up in a British victory, that he had to avoid at all costs. So he drilled his men, regiment by a regiment, trying to come up with military projects to keep them all busy. Washington needed to know one thing and one thing only – where was Henry Knox?

Washington's Savior

Chapter 5

The Naval Secretary

Now Washington had some special work for Colonel John Glover.

The siege of Boston had shown Washington the value of combining and coordinating army and navy operations to make each soldier and sailor as effective as possible. He proved it with finality at Yorktown in 1781.

Washington knew Glover was a man of the sea, and he sent Glover back to the coast for a special reason. He told him to find one or two good ships and turn them into fighting vessels that could provide some opposition to the British ships. He was to create an American navy in being.

To make things easier and quicker for all, Glover suggested they use his schooner *Hannah,* as an appropriate experimental warship. His plans were approved and the ship was tied up at Glover's wharf in Beverly for outfitting. Thus she was commissioned as the first armed ship of the rebellion.

In reality that's what it was. It wasn't in the U.S. Navy because the United States did not exist at that time. It was not the Congress' Navy because it had no idea what Washington was doing. In fact, it was really the Army's Navy, Washington's Navy.

Mystery Ship

Little is known about the *Hannah* except that she was a schooner and she displaced about 78 tons of water. The Dutch designed the first schooners in the 1550s for use in their North Sea fisheries. Much later, Atlantic fisherman from Cape Ann and Cape Gloucester enhanced those original designs for use in the Atlantic Ocean, and the *Hannah* was such a vessel.

She was probably a two or three-mast schooner, equipped with fore and aft rigging to keep the crew small and she probably carried four to six guns. On her maiden cruise, the *Hannah* captured the munitions ship *Unity*, its cargo, being invaluable for Washington in refilling his dwindling supply of powder and shot. Or so they believed.

It turned out that John Langdon of Portsmouth, N.H, the hero of Fort Constitution, owned the *Unity*. Langdon demanded the ship and its cargo be returned.

Washington, the ultimate arbitrator, agreed, and the *Hannah* lost her only prize. Her short naval career ended in October when *Hannah* ran aground on some sharp, jagged rocks outside of Beverly harbor. She survived the ordeal and went to sea again, but only as a merchant trader.

Washington's Savior

On October 4th, Glover was ordered back to the coast in short order and ordered to work there full-time. He would retain command of the troops at Cambridge, so he would have to make frequent trips between Cambridge and Beverly.

Washington also assigned Colonel Stephan Moylan, the muster-master from his staff, to accompany Glover and to support his activities. Moylan, a native Irishman, had come to the city of Philadelphia several years ago, where he had been engaged in several different businesses, including a variety of shipping and trading operations. To make things even more complicated, the General named Colonel Joseph Reed to supervise the entire naval operation. Reed was Washington's private secretary and his staff chief, and he was not above meddling in their affairs whether warranted or not.[16]

Reed often infuriated Glover, who was well known in the regiment for his quick temper and normally low tolerance of criticism. Being the head of his regiment and the owner of his own business, he was used to giving orders, not taking

---

[16] Not long after the army left Boston, Reed returned to Pennsylvania where he was elected president of the provincial Congress, essentially president of Pennsylvania. Before he left, Washington had accidentally opened a letter Reed had written to General Horatio Gates in which he heartily criticized Washington while encouraging Gates to lobby Congress for the top job. In 1778, Reed got into a furious dispute with the new military governor of Philadelphia – Major General Benedict Arnold. This dispute had much to do with Arnold eventually turning coat. Reed died in July 1786.

them. Glover would usually spout-off to the more patient Moylan, who would cool him down before he went too far.

The General had a fairly large staff which he normally kept busy all day writing, transcribing letters, and other documents Washington used as communication tools on a daily basis. In October, he finally dictated precise instructions to both men and sent them via Colonel Reed.

Col. Glover and Mr. Moylan
At Camp in Cambridge
Oct. 4, 1775

His Excellency, resolved to employ two armed vessels, has empowered you two to negotiate this business, in which the following directions are to be observed.

1st That the two vessels are to be approved are as well founded as possible.

2nd That you have an appraisement of them by indifferent people.

3rd That you agree, at as reasonable rate as you can, for the hire of the vessels, and, if possible, procure the cannon and vessels on loan, or if not, purchase them at the cheapest rate per month.

4th If you cannot find cannon or equipment at Salem or Marblehead, you may go to Newburyport, where there are several vessels available, and sundry cannons.

5th You are, as soon as possible, to write down proper directions for making the cartridges, and providing ammunition, and a list of what will you will be wanting.

6th You are to nominate some suitable person at Cape Ann, Marblehead or places where such prizes may be sent, as an agent to take care of such prizes, instructing him to give as early information as possible of all captures, and a list of cargos, as far as he can do according to the papers...and let them be persons of approved good character and of known substances. All agreements are to be put in writing.

7th All contracts entered into by you jointly, when together, or separately in case one should go to Newbury, the General will ratify and confirm.

8th As soon as either of the vessels is in such forwardness as to be ready to sail in a few days, then you are to send notice of it to Headquarters, that officers and men may march down to see it.

I am sirs, your most obedient servant,

Geo. Washington[17]

Thereafter, Glover and Moylan followed Washington's instructions to the letter. They also arranged for a well known and well–respected local man to act as Washington's agent – Glover's older brother Jonathan. It proved to be a good choice because Jonathan was an astute businessman and he kept the accounts precisely and accurately, which is what Washington wanted.

It was said that during the winter of 1775-1776 at any one time there were more than 30

---

[17] Washington to Glover, Moylan, 10/3/1775, Upham, p. 8-9.

ships riding at anchor in the American fleet in Beverly harbor.

The First Flotilla

It didn't take Glover and Moylan long to get ready for a war cruise. Captain Nicholson Broughton, former skipper of the *Hannah*, was made a commodore in command of two vessels. He skippered the schooner *Lynch*, six guns, and another captain, John Selman, was given the schooner *Franklin*, four guns. Broughton took overall command of the two-ship flotilla and they set sail on October 21, 1775. Their charge was to blockade Boston and try to capture two bothersome English warships that were wrecking havoc on American shipping near the mouth of the St. Lawrence.

Bad weather made it difficult to do anything around Boston, so Broughton turned his tiny fleet to the north. Though small, schooners are extremely seaworthy and neither captain had any qualms about taking their commands out into the real ocean. They went far afield but could not get near the St. Lawrence. Instead, they turned south and took positions off the Island of St. John's, today's Prince Edward Island.

In addition to patrolling the waters, they also landed on the island, captured a fort and brought the garrison back to Massachusetts as prisoners. In early November, Glover brought the captains, some of the crew, and most of the prisoners to Cambridge to meet with Washington.

To their joint embarrassment, Washington

was not pleased with the results of the cruise. Washington had decided to be less belligerent toward Canada and encourage uprisings against the British. This naval cruise ruined Washington's shift in strategic direction and Canada would never revolt against the Crown.

Praise not often Forthcoming

Glover was soon to learn that unsolicited praise from Washington was a very rare event. The General expected men to do their duty. If they wanted extra they should look elsewhere.

In addition, Glover would receive critical letters from Colonel Reed in which he would express Washington's displeasure, usually about with speed or lack there of, related to outfitting a specific ship.

Glover would then patiently bring either man or both up to speed as to what was causing the delay. There were usually one of two culprits – lack crew or lack of ship fitting supplies and both could be blamed on the war.

John Jr.

Something happened that caused a strain in the relations between Colonel Glover and General Washington. Early on in his naval staffing discussions, Washington had offered the command of a ship to John Glover, Jr., the Colonel's 20- year-old elder son. Now the General was having second thoughts about entrusting a ship to one so young. Glover felt somewhat betrayed by the General, but John Jr. said he would accept Washington's new idea of being second-in-command to a senior captain.

Young Glover went to sea aboard the *Hannah* serving under future brother-in-law Captain Nicholson Broughton.

After the cruise, John Jr. decided to scrap his naval career and he went back to his father's regiment, where he was a company captain. He never told any one outside the family why.

Roll Call of Naval Heroes

Several prominent naval officers got their start under Glover as privateers and captains. One such captain was John Manley. On October 28, 1775, Manley commanded the *Lee* and he captured the *Nancy*, a well stocked munitions ship whose cargo Washington put to good use during his siege of Boston.

Later, Manley commanded the frigates *Hancock* and *Hague*. He died in Boston in 1793, a naval hero.

Delivering John Adams

Another heroic captain was Samuel Tucker, also of Marblehead. Military legend at the time said that Tucker captured more British guns, seamen and ships than John Paul Jones or any other captain during the war.

Tucker was also the captain who took John Adams to Europe in 1779 on board the American frigate *Boston*. During that voyage, they fell in with a British warship. Adams knew his capture meant a trial for treason, a probable public execution in front of cheering crowds at the Tower of London, or at Execution Dock along the River Thames. This was the execution site for the famous pirate from the colony of New York – Captain William Kidd – several decades earlier. After Kidd's death, his body was hung in a cage on a gibbet on the dock and it took several years for it to rot away to nothingness.

Adams agreed to go below and remain there while the two ships fought. However, minutes later Tucker saw Adams trying to fight the enemy with only a musket. The two argued over Adams exposure on deck and he finally agreed to go below. He and his son John Quincy Adams arrived safely in France – two future presidents of the United States.

One of the most famous victories of the Beverly Navy came on May 16th, 1776. Captain James Mugford was patrolling Boston harbor in a Glover ship crewed by twenty soldiers from the regiment when he captured a munitions brig. When they got the ship back to the dock and examined the cargo, they found the ship contained more than 1,500 barrels of gunpowder and hundreds of other items of munitions – items sorely needed by the Continental Army. Washington called this one of the most valuable sea captures of the war.

Washington tells the Congress

Washington's Savior

On October 5, Washington told Congress about his naval activities and received approval to keep the operation in business. All told, the Beverly operation under Glover and Moylan was probably a more successful naval office than most handled by sovereign nations. Glover and Moylan bought, sold, and managed ships; hired and fired crews; handled ship fittings with things like riggings and sails; and acted as ships' chandlers.

Facts tell the story of the impact Washington's navy had on the war. They also gave an indication of Glover's effectiveness while he served as Washington's secretary of the navy. From May, 1775 to February, 1778, more than 73 American-flagged privateers left ports throughout New England and they captured a total of 730 vessels valued at more than twenty million pounds.

During this time, Congress also became interested in naval affairs. In fact, they set up a special naval committee to determine to look into the operations of the navy and began the steps needed to lay the keel for the real United States Navy.

Freshwater fleets

Further north and unknown to Washington and Glover, another makeshift navy was being constructed in the woods of New York State and on the shores of Lake Champlain. For there Benedict Arnold was building ships to beat a

British army if it tried to come down from Canada.

Arnold was the Connecticut officer who, along with Ethan Allen and his Green Mountain Boys, had captured Fort Ticonderoga in May of 1775. Not only would the fort provide the cannon that Henry Knox would use to end the siege of Boston, but the gray stone fortress would remain a target for the two armies as they battled in the Adirondack forest for supremacy.

In the spring, the British followed Arnold out of Canada. Arnold felt he could not defeat Governor Guy Carleton's army with his own 'rabble in arms.' But he hoped he could delay the arrival of the British on Lake Champlain – the highway to Albany in the 18th century – with a navy. His veteran woodsmen got to work with their axes and the fleet began to take shape. Also, it didn't take long for Carlton to realize what was going on. He stopped his men on the shore of the lake, and began to build his own fleet. Carlton already knew the value of the lake – he brought several disassembled vessels hat his men simply put back together.

The fleets finally took to the water on October 11 and both sides cleared the decks for battle. Arnold had about a dozen ships including a sloop and a schooner, but most of the ships were gundalows – simple flat bottom boats that could carry one cannon mounted on the bow.

The two fleets met off Valcour Island in a running lake battle that lasted most of the day. It was a disaster – half of Arnold's ships were sunk. The rest were trapped in a small inlet on the

Vermont shore. The entrance was completely blocked by Carlton's fleet.

But Arnold would not be trapped. As the mist formed on the lake that evening, Arnold had his men muffle their oars and oarlocks and the remnants of the fleet began to move slowly past the British who never saw them leave. When Carlton woke up the Americans were gone.

Carlton now knew he had no choice but to withdraw. It was too late in the season, the snows would start soon and his army had no winter quarters.

The fleet and army went back to Canada. It would return next year to a village called Saratoga.

Chapter 6

To Independence

In the fall of 1775, Glover and Moylan were commuting between Cambridge and the coast as they worked to put the naval force together. That was soon altered after several British frigates began to raid the American shore facilities at Marblehead and Beverly.

Washington decided to counter those incursions by reassigning the 23rd rRegiment back to its home area of Marblehead and Beverly. That ended Glover's commute but he would make sure he went back to Cambridge often enough to know what was going on there.

They also got a new identity. The 23rd Massachusetts became the 14th Massachusetts Continental Regiment.

Meanwhile Washington and the rest of the army began to wonder where was Henry Knox?

They knew he had arrived safely at Ticonderoga and had left several weeks' later, disassembled cannon on board newly built sledges to run on the ice of Lake George and the snow of New England. Then they disappeared into the hard winter of the Berkshire Mountains of western Massachusetts.

Finally, Glover was in Cambridge when news arrived on January 20, 1776, that Knox was just twenty miles away. Washington quashed any celebration in case General Howe should get wind of their good fortune.

The remaining weeks of the siege of Boston were anti-climatic. Knox delivered 59 cannon of various sizes, which were reassembled by the artillery teams who would handle them. Washington had already selected a place for the guns. They would go on the crest of Dorchester Heights, an elevated ridge which even today overlooks the town and the harbor. Guns there would mean the British would have to leave.

To be truly effective, however, guns like those Knox delivered needed defensive works where riflemen and infantry could protect them and their gun crews from frontal or flank assault.

Washington and staff met again to plan the next step. He proposed to test the temper of his army by making a frontal assault on Boston. But his officers protested against that idea, saying he had not seen the carnage at Bunker Hill, but they had and they would counsel no such repeat of that day. They voted that the siege would now become an artillery barrage.

One thing George Washington had, was a great capacity of patience; he was willing to listen, take advice, and to carry out other's plans and advice that superseded his own. But only to a certain extent. As a general, he understood the need to get others' opinions, but he also knew the need to carry out his own ideas. Washington believed the Army could not survive as a democracy – soon the election of officers would have to end once and for all.

Washington's Savior

Colonial Prefab

What they did now was most unusual – the Continental Army spent the next several weeks pre-fabricating the gun emplacements. They built them at the bottom of their side of Dorchester Heights. Then, as soon as the sun went down on March 5th, 1776, they worked until dawn broke to get them in place. Every man in the entire army worked on the project, as well as many volunteer citizens and as many volunteers as they could find.

The next morning, General Howe woke up and saw the guns glowering down at him. Instantly, he knew two things. He knew, as he told his staff, "Those men did more work in one night than my men could have done in three months."[18]

The second thing he knew was that he had to leave Boston. The guns had forced him out without a fight. And that was a good thing because he was unaware that the Americans did not have enough shot and powder to fight with them. Howe's spies had failed to uncover that important fact.

Howe tried to bombard the guns using shipboard artillery to no avail, and a planned landing on the mainland failed because of bad weather. Finally, Howe had to ask Washington for a truce – basically asking for permission to go.

Washington told General Howe they could leave on March 17th – it would be the only day

---

[18] Scheer and Rankin., p. 117.

that would do.

Dual Holiday

March 17th is a dual holiday in today's Boston, Massachusetts. Of course it is St. Patrick's Day as all good Irish know and there were and still are a many good Irish in Boston. Boston's St. Patrick's Day celebration is legendary throughout the world.

March 17th is also Evacuation Day for Suffolk County, which is today's city of Boston. The date is still recognized today, although in 2009 the state legislature did attempt to eradicate Bunker Hill Day from the list of state and local holiday. Proponents of the measure claimed they were archaic holidays that held no value for modern day New Englanders. And besides the Commonwealth would save money in holiday pay. But old holidays must have meaning for some people because the measure failed to pass muster on Beacon Hill. The holidays remain on the books in Massachusetts.

For days prior to March 17th, soldiers on the hillsides surrounding Boston peered into the city and watched the activities as the people there got ready to leave. Washington warned Howe not to loot the town but Howe did not stop the Loyalists from taking whatever they wished to from houses in Boston. The Loyalists had lost everything they owned when they abandoned their homes outside of the then-provincial capital after Lexington and Concord. There was no going back for either side.

In fact, Massachusetts would move quickly to deal with Loyalists and the remnants of their property. In 1777, the state legislature passed the Massachusetts Confiscation Act that took all property and possessions left behind by the Loyalists. No one would get anything back.

On March 17th, Howe's ships – more than one hundred of them – weighed anchor, disappeared among dozens of the harbor islands, then found the main channel again and set out to sea. One by one, they left, leaving the harbor empty of all shipping flying the Union Jack.

No doubt thousands of soldiers and probably most of the Loyalists watched as the ships left Boston carrying friends and relatives they probably would never see again.

The lobsters were gone.

Praise the Lord.

Boston was free at last.

Washington watched all this with optimism, but he allowed no celebration or triumphant entries into the town. He knew what kind of victory this was and he refused to celebrate.

He ordered several regiments into the town to prevent mob rule and any possible looting. The rebel flag flew over the Custom House in Boston as the last British ship left the harbor.

Over in Boston

Boston was free, and, although no one

knew it at the time, the Revolution was over in New England. It was only March 1776, months *before* Independence. But the work for most of the leading revolutionaries, like Sam Adams, John Hancock, and Paul Revere, was almost all done. That trio would play but minor roles in the rest of the drama.

Now the revolution born and nurtured in Boston would be taken over by other men in the southern part of the colonies, in the central states and from Pennsylvania and New Jersey and New York and from Virginia. Boston remained THE cradle of liberty but it would be one without military problems for the rest of war.

Washington himself was quite pleased with the victory. Boston was simply a matter of time; other battles would be a matter of fighting.

Washington was also anxious to leave and move to the next dangerous location – New York City. There was slight delay in the movement south, however, when it was reported General Howe had anchored off Nantasket Roads, some five miles to the south of the town. Howe's Fleet stayed there for about 10 days, then they left, destination Halifax.

By April 3rd, George Washington was ready to move. He left General Ward in charge of Boston and left five good militia regiments with him. He was awarded an honorary degree from Harvard University and it was a distinction he always treasured. He also made plans for John Glover. Glover had done good work at Beverly, and he knew more could be done if he had more time there. Congress agreed.

As a result, Glover and his 14th Continentals would be the only regular army unit left in New England. But he would not be there long – Washington said, telling Glover to wait for word from New York. They would be needed.

Independence

Much further south in the city of Philadelphia, forces were working on another major issue that would impact everyone in the Continental Army and in the thirteen colonies – independence.

The effort under way in the spring of 1776 was the second try, an earlier attempt being foiled by more moderate forces led by John Dickinson of Pennsylvania. One of the driving forces behind the issue was John Adams of Massachusetts, who strongly felt it was time to sever the formal connections between the colonies and England. It took so long to debate the issues that the vote on independence wasn't taken until July 2nd, and even then the issues were still in doubt.

Richard Henry Lee of Virginia made the motion and John Adams seconded it. This was an example of Virginia and Massachusetts – the two oldest and largest of colonies, working together.

Now the Roll Call

New Hampshire	Yea
Massachusetts	Yea
Rhode Island	Yea

Washington's Savior

Connecticut	Yea
New York	Abstains
New Jersey	Yea

A disruption as Delaware Delegate
    Caesar Rodney carried into hall

Delaware	Yea
Maryland	Yea
Virginia	Yea
North Carolina	Yea
South Carolina	Yea
Georgia.	Yea

It was over. They were free. It was done. Delegates looked each other, as if to say what do we do now. No one knew.

The vote was 12-0 with one abstention. However within several days New York was able to change its vote to yes. That made it truly unanimous.

On July 2nd, 1776 the Declaration of Independence was read, annotated, and approved by the Second Continental Congress. A clean copy was sent to King George III to let him know what his American colonies, or former colonies, were doing.

What they did was to create a real war; it was no longer an insurgency or a conflict between neighbors and brothers. This was war, deadly war. It would pit thirteen small colonies united together for safety sake, if nothing else, against the world's largest empire and it would truly be an amazing story.

Washington's Savior

An ecstatic John Adams knew they had done the right thing. Jubilantly, he wrote a prophetic letter to his wife Abigail:

> The second day of July, 1776 will be the most epochal moment in the history of America. I am apt to believe they will be celebrated by succeeding generations as the great anniversary festival. It ought to be might be commemorated as a day of deliverance, by solemn acts of devotion to all God Almighty. It ought to be solemnized with pomp and parade, with shows, games, sports, guns, bells, bonfires and illuminations, from one end of this continent to the other, from this time forward forevermore.
>
> You will think me transported with enthusiasm, but I am not. I am well aware of the toil in blood and treasure that it will cost us to maintain this declaration in support defending states yet, through all the gloom, I can see the rays and ravishing light and glory. I can see the end is more than worth all the means. And that posterity will triumph in that day's transaction, even though we should rue it, which I trust in God shall not.[19]

In retrospect, Adams did an excellent job of describing future Fourth of July celebrations. The only thing he got wrong was the date.

Heard for the First Time

Normally a good quiet, taciturn man, Glover seemed almost animated in his excitement that morning in early July when he mustered his entire regiment in Beverly. Families were there

---

[19] Scheer & Rankin, p. 151.

too.

He made small talk with several officers and he congratulated a number of men who had recent additions to their families.

Finally he called the regiment to attention. He said he brought them greetings and good wishes from General Washington in New York and he said the General had asked him to read a special document to them.

He then unfolded the paper and began to read the words so carefully chosen by Thomas Jefferson.

"When in the course of human events it becomes necessary..."

They all listened intently for the first time to the Declaration of Independence.

BOOK TWO

NEW YORK - 1776

Washington had to learn how to lose before he could learn how to win. The battles for New York were his "university of losing." The lessons at the hands of the British and Hessians were harsh, but he earned his Ph. D. on Manhattan. He saved the Revolution.

But the lessons there would haunt him for the rest of his life.

As for John Glover, the next six months would change him in ways he had never imagined. It was during the battles for New York that John Glover became known as the man from Massachusetts who saved the Revolution and its leader.

Chapter 7

The War Goes South

On July 11, John Glover mustered his regiment on the parade ground in Beverly. His speech was short and to the point – General Washington needed the 14th Continentals in New York and he needed them as soon as possible. They would leave on July 20th.

By August 9th, the more than five hundred members of the 14th Continental regiment from Marblehead had trudged 250 miles through an equally dusty and dirty New England and, had passed through the picket lines to rejoin the Continental Army of the United States of America.

They had walked through a vital part of the new country they had vowed to defend, as province blended into province, or since independence was declared, state blended into state. Many of the Marblehead boys had never left their hometown by land – many had seen other shores through their seagoing work as fishermen or merchant traders.

They walked military-fashion, tightly disciplined, and they held their heads high as they marched through the countryside toward Boston.

Walking Through New England

They circumvented the town, moving through the abandoned siege works, from which they could look down on the tired town. Ships were moored to docks throughout the harbor – Long Wharf was especially busy, with ships waiting nearby for a dock space. Boston was recovering itself as a port.

And the 14th Massachusetts Continentals marched south along the great post road that led past the large frame house and farm, near Braintree, that John Adams called home and where his wife, Abigail, continued to raise their children and write the letters that so bolstered and inspired him while he served in the Congress at Philadelphia.

South

Many people along the route would give the men water or even some fruits or vegetables that were ripening. This was their way of thanking these young men for helping free the colonies.

South

Many other farmers feared this or any marching army – especially isolated units like the 14th – would loot their farms and take all of their livestock and other foodstuffs. They were afraid the soldiers would burn their fields and buildings, especially. But there was nothing to fear from the 14th for all American army units were under strict orders from Washington to pay for everything they took from civilians.

Washington's Savior

South

Massachusetts blended into Rhode Island as the regiment continued south. They saw the church spires of Providence in the distance and then they touched on Narragansett Bay. No doubt many of the soldiers wished they could appropriate some of the empty boats and ships they passed so they could sail to New York rather than walk. It was very hot and the dust rose as they marched.

South

Several days later, they crossed the line between Rhode Island and Connecticut and saw the land here was a little bit different from their own state. It was less hilly, perhaps less rocky, perhaps easier to farm. But still it wasn't home.

South

As they marched closer to New York, they moved to the south to walk along the cooler Long Island Sound. The 'Yorkers' who lived there were none too friendly and many houses and farms were shuttered up as they went by. The rumors were this was Tory country and most people here were still loyal to the King.

On the evening of August 8th, Glover told his men to clean their uniforms and prepare themselves for their arrival the following morning in the camp of the Continental Army. Fires glowed throughout their campsite as the men washed their clothes and hung them up to dry. They also cleaned firearms, sharpened their swords and knives, and cleaned up the powder horns.

They tied their hair in a traditional queue or just cut it to a uniform length. Glover was determined the 14th would make a good impression with Washington and the men wanted to do the same thing after the long and dusty walk.

As the sun came up, Glover formed his regiment so they could move out at sunrise. Within an hour they were approaching Washington's lines. Glover and his adjutant went forward, crossed the East River in a small boat and soon were at Washington's headquarters, here as in Boston, in an abandoned loyalist mansion.

During a brief interview, Washington told Glover he would be part of General Fellows' Brigade, which in turn was part of Sullivan's division. The other units of Fellows Brigade were militia units from Worcester, Bristol, and Berkshire counties of Massachusetts.

General John Sullivan

Glover nodded. He knew John Fellows and he especially knew John Sullivan, a lawyer from Durham, New Hampshire, who had also served in the Continental Congress before leading troops at Boston. Before the siege was lifted, Sullivan had been sent to Canada to command troops there after defeats in the north.

At best a mediocre general, Sullivan commanded several divisions for Washington in various campaigns and also held independent commands later in the war. Sullivan was extremely loyal to George Washington throughout the war, Washington rarely forgot his friends.

Sullivan told Glover the defensive situation in New York was difficult at best. While Washington had been in Boston, General Charles Lee was responsible for the defenses of New York. But Congress soon sent Lee to Charleston, South Carolina, to handle the defenses there.

When Washington returned to New York, little had been done. And after Howe and his army arrived in early July, the Continentals spent most of its time shadowing the British and trying to fathom their plans.

Sullivan said the bulk of the army was divided between Long Island and Manhattan. On Long Island, there were 9,000 troops defending the works on Brooklyn Heights. Another similar force was scattered throughout Manhattan. And Glover would soon find out for himself, how confusing the command was in New York City. Shortly after his arrival, Sullivan was given a new assignment and the defense of Brooklyn was passed over to Major General Israel Putnam of Connecticut.

'Old Put' in 1776 was a 58-year-old gentleman farmer and soldier who was a veteran of the French and Indian Wars. Washington would soon discover that Putnam was past his prime as a soldier, but he was encouraged by Congress to keep him in command to placate the Connecticut members of Congress.

Dive, Dive, Dive

The new United States might not have much of a Navy in New York harbor in 1776, but it did have a revolutionary naval weapon. David Bushnell of Connecticut had designed and built the world's first working submarine, and he was determined to try it out on the British Navy. On August 6th, the round wooden vessel called *The Turtle* made its way into the harbor and moved towards the British fleet.

The Turtle's weapon was really a drill that the one-man crew would use to make a hole in the hull, and then attach an explosive charge on a long fuse. Unfortunately, when *The Turtle* attempted to torpedo the flagship of Admiral Howe, the copper bottom of the vessel repulsed it. Bushnell apparently forgot the British used the copper sheathing to retard the growth of vegetation on the wooden hulls of their ships.

Fire

Things were quiet for Colonel John Glover and his men for several weeks after the 14th Continentals arrived in New York, but at least one of his officers seemed to have been involved in a special August incident.

Admiral Lord Richard Howe, the General's brother, had been trying to find ways to bring some of the power of his ships to bear on the Americans. He decided to use two of his frigates, the HMS *Phoenix,* 35 guns, and the HMS *Rose,* 25 guns, in as many ways as possible as often as he could. In August, he sent the ships through the artillery gauntlet Henry Knox had set up along the Hudson. The two ships raised their anchors, slipped out into the stream, and turned about north up the Hudson.

Going upriver, the frigates hugged the New Jersey bank and they easily made their way past a series of heavily engaged gun batteries. Knox's guns hit the ships many times but did absolutely no damage. Admiral Howe ordered his ships to stay north of Manhattan and the two dropped anchor up river near Tarrytown, NY.

Washington was livid when he heard what happened. It was embarrassing for his artillery to fail like that and he refused to talk about this for several days. And when he did, he wanted revenge.

On August 16th, two small skiffs left a cove at the tip of Manhattan and headed toward the moored frigates. Each vessel was full of branches, logs, brush, paper, cloth, cordage – and anything else that would ignite and burn – soaked in pitch, tar and oil. But these were not ordinary river skiffs – they were fire ships.

Throughout the age of fighting sail – 1770 through 1815 – few weapons caused so much fear and terror in the hearts of officers and crew than a fire ship. A naval vessel then was a mass of wood, cloth, fibers and oceans of flammable resins, making them powder kegs that once ignited, may never have gone out.

That August day, the one-man crews ignited their vessels and then aimed them squarely at the British ships. When they were close enough, each man jumped overboard and swam away. A third boat that followed the fire ships picked up each man and brought him away to safety.

The first skiff missed the *Rose*, and drifted away to burn out in the river. The second fire ship ran directly into the *Phoenix*, but that ship's crew was able to push it away before anything ignited. The fire ships had failed. But they did succeed in burning the *Phoenix's* tender.

The fire ships may have failed in their primary mission, but they did get the frigates out of Tarrytown. The next day Admiral Howe had the *Phoenix* and the *Rose* leave their moorings and return to the fleet.

What is interesting about this incident is that at least one of the men who sailed the fire ships, was from Glover's 14th Regiment. Captain Thomas Fosdick was one of the Marblehead soldiers and he would serve as the adjutant of Glover's Brigade in 1778 and eventually would rise to brigade major by the end of the war. He seemed to have been close to Glover and it is true the maiden name of Glover's second wife was Fosdick, although there is no evidence that the two were related. Fosdick was the one who had sent his fire ship into the hull of the *Phoenix*.

Of the other fire ship captain – allegedly

named Thomas – we have no more information.[20]

Fosdick's name crops up again in June 1777 when Glover returns to the army just before the forces gather for what ultimately becomes the battle of Saratoga. In a letter to Washington, he recommended Fosdick to the General as a young man with intelligence, strength and high moral fiber. There is no indication that the General ever acted upon Glover's recommendation.

Chapter 8

East River Crossing

John Glover was awakened early on the morning of August 27th; in fact, he was up before dawn. His adjutant handed him a sealed envelope – orders at last. He ripped it open.

He was ordered to embark his men in boats and cross the East River to support operations in Brooklyn, as soon as possible.

Colonel John Glover had been listening to the fighting for a day and a half now, ever since it was pushed back to Brooklyn Heights. He and his men had been itching to join the fighting, but they had to wait for orders.

It sounded louder now. Glover wondered what they had been listening to for the past two

---

[20] Upham, p. 16. This is a minor controversy in the Glover story. Some historians think a different Fosdick sailed the fire ship, Upham insists this is the same Fosdick who was on Glover's roster.

days. Then it struck him – it was very simple. He had been listening to the near annihilation of the Continental Army.

Howe vs. Washington

Howe arrived off Sandy Hook, New York City's mooring location on June 23rd. On July 12th, his brother, Admiral Richard Howe arrived with 100 warships and transports full of soldiers and supplies. In early August, Sir Henry Clinton arrived from South Carolina. All told, the British had a fleet of 427 transports and 52 warships floating in New York harbor. At that point in time, there were more than 32,000 well-trained and well-equipped British and Hessian soldiers waiting to land and face some 17,000 troops – mainly untrained and untested – in the Continental Army.

George Washington had fortified Brooklyn Heights, which dominated New York City across the East River, much as Dorchester Heights had dominated Boston. General Howe also tried to begin negotiations with the Americans, perhaps hoping to end the war that way. But the Declaration of Independence had done its work in fortifying the Americans to keep their hopes of freedom alive, and the potential for peace talks, always Howe's preference to war, came to naught.

On August 24th, General Howe began the operation that he felt would quickly smash the Americans and their revolt. Howe and a large portion of the British army were ferried across New York harbor from Staten Island to Gravesend

Washington's Savior

Bay on Long Island.

The landings were unopposed.

The British General later said they were greeted like conquerors, warmly welcomed by villagers who gave them food and drink. Long Island Tories were mainly of Germanic origin and they were totally loyal to the King.

That day, General Putnam engaged the British and he was steadily driven back by the red-coated foe. They were still some distance from Brooklyn Heights when both sides rested on the evening of the 26th.

Toward evening an intelligence report from Tory sympathizers let Howe know that one of the four passes through the Heights of Guana, the ridge that separates Brooklyn from the rest of Long island – the Jamaica Pass – was either unguarded or lightly patrolled.

Howe questioned the Tories and then conferred with his generals. After pouring over several maps, Howe developed his strategy – often credited to Henry Clinton – and gave his orders. Several hours after nightfall, Generals Howe, Clinton, and Cornwallis led more than 14,000 soldiers out into the night. General James Grant was told to assault the American lines in the morning.

Shortly after dawn, Grant, who deeply despised the American revolutionaries, renewed the fighting with Putnam's men. Both sides fought hard and determinedly, the rebels holding their ground and fighting well against a superior force.

Washington's Savior
Rolling Them Up

Then, at about 9 A.M., the Continentals heard sounds and then cannon fire ***behind*** them. When they looked to see what it was, they saw a nightmare on the move – lines of red-coated British and dark-coated German soldiers attacking their rear, moving in their direction, with bayonets fixed. Howe and his 14,000 troops had marched all night and rolled up a small guard Putnam had left at the Jamaica Pass. Then they moved in quickly to try and get the rebels in a classic double envelopment.

Trapped between two attacking British forces, the Continentals had only one recourse open to most of them – to run. And run they did. Those young farm boys dropped their muskets, and ran.

They ran past their officers, they ran past their generals. They ran until the river stopped them.

Meanwhile, General Howe was gathering his prisoners back at the Brooklyn Heights works. By the time they were done, the British captured more than 400; another 1,000 soldiers were killed or wounded. Three American generals – Israel Putnam, John Sullivan, and William Alexander, who was also known as Lord Stirling, a Scottish title that was claimed by his family – were taken along with a rebel baggage train. General Howe was very satisfied.

Down and Out in Brooklyn

Washington's Savior

As he left the riverbank that morning, Colonel Glover roused his men to prepare for battle. There seemed to be a burning ache in his gut telling him today was not going to be a good day. Glover paced his lines all day, talking to his men, encouraging them, watching the river and waiting for a call to action by Israel Putnam, a call that never came.

General Washington had left the Manhattan camp at about 2 P.M. with 2,000 men. Rumor had it that Putnam and Sullivan had been captured and most of the army was but a shout from Howe away from capture.

Finally, Glover got his orders at about 5 A.M. the next day. As quickly as he could, he got his men across the river and into new defensive lines around Wallabout Bay, on the north end of the perimeter along the East River. Right then about 9,500 men of the Continental Army were trapped on a speck of land one mile deep and two miles long, with their backs to the East River.

Washington Decides

Washington had seemed to bumble away the 27th but by the 28th he knew where safety lay – a mile across the East River on Manhattan Island. He realized he had to evacuate Long Island and get all his troops back to Manhattan.

The British had captured Major General John Sullivan and they decide to turn the former New Hampshire lawyer into a messenger. Sullivan was sent back through American lines to tell Washington, Howe wanted to begin peace talks, but the Virginian had no interest.

Washington held a conference with his staff and key officers, and explained the situation. They were in extreme danger and the only thing protecting them now was the weather and that eventually would change to favor Howe, too.

Their safety valve was the driving rain from the nor'easter that had arrived that afternoon. It would cover the move from the enemy and should keep Admiral Howe's ships at anchor and away from the East River.

Quartermasters had already collected all of the small boats they could find on the side of the river. Brigadier General Thomas Mifflin's men would form the rear guard and would occupy the perimeter defenses while the rest of the army skee-daddled. General Alexander McDougall, a New York City merchant turned soldier, would be in charge of the embarkation of the men in the boats.

Essex County Mariners

Then Washington called upon two more men. The first was John Glover, Colonel of the 14th Massachusetts, leader of the men from Marblehead. The second was Colonel Israel Hutchinson, leader of the 27th Massachusetts, whose men were from Salem, Beverly, and Danvers.

Both regiments were from Essex County, Massachusetts, and were highly respected for their ability to handle small boats in any kind of weather. Both men would work with McDougal to make sure all the troops were across the river before sunrise.[21]

Both colonels went back to their regiments and told the men what they had to do. As the rainy cloak of night fell, the men slipped out of their defensive positions and marched to the river to begin the rowing. Various groups of soldiers also made camp sounds throughout the night so Howe wouldn't catch on.

George Washington and his Allies

George Washington had three distinct allies in his effort to get across the East River and save his army after the Battle of Brooklyn, or Long Island. His essential allies were:

1. **General Howe**. The British commander had many chances to totally annihilate Washington during the New York campaign, yet no opportunity was a good as this one at the East River. A simple assault was all that was needed. A good push and the revolt would be over. But Howe, as before, was still haunted by Bunker Hill and he

---

[21] Many contemporary and modern narratives about the evacuation of Brooklyn do not even mention the participation of the 27th Massachusetts I don't know why. Glover seems to get all of the glory for this work, but it was really a team effort between the two regiments. Perhaps Glover won the public relation wars. Other accounts and histories mention Glover and his 'Cape Cod' not Cape Ann fishermen. There is a major difference between the two capes. The residents of each will tell you in no uncertain terms.

would not attack.

2. **The weather**. Washington should and probably did bless that nor'easter. Without it, the revolution would have been over. And the fog...wow.

3. **Massachusetts**, especially Essex County. Without the small boat skills of those two regiments from that tiny county, they never would have crossed.

Saving the Army

William Upham, in his 1863 memoir of Colonel Glover, starts the tale of the effort:

> Colonel Glover went over from New York to superintend transportation; at about seven in the evening, officers and men went to work with the spirit and resolution peculiar to the Marblehead corps. The oars were muffled and everything was done with the greatest possible silence and dispatch[22].

Now it was a race against the clock. Glover figured they had to be done by 6 A.M. If they were not gone by then, they would be in for a tough fight with the British.

But now the weather, their great protector, became a problem. It wasn't just raining – sheets of water were pouring down, drenching everybody. It was quickly filling the boats, so

---

[22] Upham, p 12.

quickly in fact that several boats had to return to shore so fast that soldiers almost had to bail out the boats as they rowed.

In addition, the river was becoming choppy and rough, and the waves, white caps, and seasickness were making some of the one-mile trips across the East River pure Hell. Washington talked to Glover and MacDougall about suspending the effort. They both told Washington they had to go on. There was no choice. It was tonight or never.

By eleven P.M., however, Mother Nature had enlisted on the side of the Continentals. The wind died down gradually, then it turned to the south, making easier to get their sail boats on the river and working. The surface of the river smoothed over and allowing Glover and Hutchinson to fill the boats to their gunwales. Indeed the two colonels were filling the boat so full that water often came in over the tops.

This was no easy task for the boatmen. They had to work wet and in the rain; they had no lights to see in the fog as several groups of boats took off at once. A noise or a crash would have been fatal so they couldn't even talk in the river. And there were so many men who had crossed.

Some noises were accidental. Colonel Henry Knox was waiting on the riverbank with Glover to load a battery of cannon when one of the guns fired by mistake. The blast did no harm – the British totally ignored it, but it mortified the young and sensitive Colonel Knox and it eternally amused Colonel Glover.

Washington's Savior

Some of Glover and Hutchinson's men made as many as eleven round-trips during the long night. That meant these men rowed without food or rest for eleven rough miles. They were the true heroes of the crossing.

Glover watched his men as they rowed. They used long, strong, powerful strokes. They knew how to row in all kinds of weather and that helped that night as the surface of the river changed dramatically. They showed no emotion as they rowed; they concentrated on the river.

The men said little as they rowed. They rowed and unloaded group after group of men. Glover was pleased to see the mass of men on the Brooklyn shore getting smaller and as more and more trips were completed.

Glover continued to watch his men as they rowed back and forth across the river. He knew this was drudgework for them; awfully hard work; not the kind of work they had signed-up for. He hoped Washington, would remember that his men were first and foremost soldiers and not sailors; they had come to fight and not to row.

Leading from the Front

One thing most of the officers wanted was to get Washington back to New York and safety as quickly as possible. The last thing they wanted was to have him captured by the British in some surprise early morning attack. His staff and other officers would encourage his departure, but he would have no part of it. Instead, he would walk among his men, providing encouragement and telling them they would soon all be safe.

One officer who shared the concerns about Washington was Major Benjamin Tallmadge from a Connecticut regiment. At one point, Tallmadge could not find Washington anywhere, so he just assumed the General, seeing that things were going so well, must have taken a boat to Manhattan. He assumed he had finally gone to the other side.

Several hours later, however, Tallmadge was embarking on one of the last boats to leave, when he saw a tall figure walk out of the shadows and get into a small craft.

The General had been there all the time.

Washington's Fog

The Americans were losing the race with time. Knowing they would be about an hour short, Glover and Hutchinson tried to urge their men on as much as they could.

Around 4:00 A.M., the rain subsided but almost simultaneously a New York fog bank rolled in and covered both sides of the river with its thick, wet, sticky dampness. It also covered the East River and made it increasingly impossible for Admiral Howe to support his brother by controlling the length of the waterway with his warships.

By 5:00 A.M., however, the fog was burning off as the sun began to rise on the New York side. But the damp cloying fog that kept the British in their lines in Brooklyn; it remained a pea soup on Long Island. Eventually this fog would succumb to the sun as well, but it gave the Americans the extra time they needed.

Shortly after seven o'clock in the morning the last four boats pushed off from the Brooklyn bank. As the boats disappeared into the fog, Colonel Glover, who was in one of them, thought he saw British redcoats approaching the bank they had just left. It was too little too late.

Three of those four boats made it safely across the East River. The fourth didn't get away fast enough – they were 'sunshine patriots' who were trying to loot what was left of the Continental's camp. The British caught them and they probably ended up in the ghastly prison hulks that the British would keep at Wallabout Bay for the duration of this war.[23]

There will be a Tomorrow

The next morning, after the salvation by boat and oar, the Americans took stock of their situation. They had suffered a terrible defeat after which they conducted a masterful retreat, saved the Continental Army, saved George Washington, and saved the Revolution. It saved 9,500 American soldiers, and just as importantly, the guns and equipment for these men who now had lived to fight another day.

The army rejoiced when the last boatload of

---

[23] Prison hulks were the putrid remains of old warships that were cut down and refitted for the use as floating prisons. Conditions on them were generally horrible, and they were great incubators of disease. Thousands of Americans died as captives on these ships during the Revolution.

soldiers landed in New York. But when this euphoria subsided, no one had to tell Washington how lucky he was. In reality, this was not a victory, it was a postponement. And no doubt Howe would look for a speedy rematch.

General Israel Putnam said later of Howe – "General Howe is either our friend or no general. He had our whole army in his power...and yet he allowed us to escape without the least interruption."

William Upham wrote in 1863 – "This event, one of the most remarkable the war, did much towards establishing the fame of Washington. It would, however, have been impossible but for the skill and activity of Glover and his Marblehead mariners."[24]   Others   agreed. Nathan Sanborn wrote in 1903 "the perfect success of the evacuation of Long Island by the Continental Army...was due to the sailor-soldiers of Glover's regiment."[25]

The British reaction was mixed. Howe was amazed the Americans could move so quickly to get things done: but then he was still impressed with what they had done at Dorchester Heights.

Ambrose Serle, Admiral Howe's private secretary, thought the only thing the Continental Army could do better than the British was run.

It did not take long for Washington to recognize John Glover for his contributions to the survival of the Army. On September 4th, 1776, in a salute to his ability and gallantry under fire, Colonel John Glover was given command of a

---

[24] Upham, p. 13
[25] Sanborn, p. 21.

brigade, a definite increase in responsibility but not a promotion in rank.

Not yet.

Chapter 9

March and Fight; Fight and March

The rank and file of the Continental Army rested after the East River withdrawal.

They were tired, battered and many were fed up with soldiering. Hundreds slipped away when their officers were not looking and most of them had no intention of ever coming back to that cursed army.

The American high command met shortly after their narrow escape to discuss their next move. They were all united in the opinion that New York was not defensible without a navy. Their forces were too scattered and they needed to concentrate on the army again. Some of them wanted to hear from Congress.

They all felt that General Howe would soon try to avenge himself on the Americans for their escape from Brooklyn.

Major General Nathanael Greene said they could just burn the damn city to the ground. Charles Lee agreed, and he was not alone among senior generals.[26] They all felt the city should be abandoned.

---

[26] There was a major fire that burned much of the city, but it happened after the Americans withdrew from New York.

Washington's Savior

But Washington said before that could be done, the army needed to evacuate some 500 wounded men across the harbor to safety in New Jersey. It was a job tailor-made for John Glover and his web-footed warriors.

Brigade commander

John Glover was getting used to a large command and larger responsibilities. He had been given General George Clinton's Brigade, which instantly became known as Glover's Brigade. But Clinton was a New Yorker and so were most of his men, and they recoiled at having a New Englander in charge.

After the inevitable reorganization, the new brigade included:

1. Glover's 14th Massachusetts;
2. The 3rd Massachusetts of Colonel William Shepherd;
3. The 19th Connecticut regiment of Colonel Charles Webb;
4. The 23rd Regiment Massachusetts of Colonel Charles Bailey;
5. and the 26th Massachusetts commanded by Colonel Loammi Baldwin.[27]

Glover certainly was pleased with his ascent to higher command, but it also brought additional problems for the man from Marblehead. Before this, Glover was able to

_____

[27] A multi-talented man, he also developed the Baldwin apple.

organize and manage his regiment quite easily. Now he had many more people for whom he was responsible.

Huts

That made his work much more difficult and early on, he did indeed show some command immaturity.

On September 28th, 1776, Glover wrote to George Washington about the state of his brigade. At one point, he mentioned that Colonel Baldwin was in desperate need of tents and wondered what Washington could do to help.

Washington no doubt had a lot more important things to think about. He was curt in his reply to John Glover. He regretted "the inconveniences Colonel Baldwin's regiment must of necessity be exposed to, but one senses a circumstance I can only lament but cannot remedy; to supply them from this place is altogether out of my power, as one half of the brigades here are the same situation...The building of huts is the most convenient manner to answer the present purpose."[28]

Baldwin's men built huts.

A Letter-Writing Man

Like most men and the few women of that era who had the chance to learn to read and write, Glover maintained letter-writing relationships with relatives and friends in

---

[28] Washington to Glover, 9/28/1776, Upham, p. 16.

Marblehead and other locations. A number of these letters have survived the passage of time and the sometimes destructive instincts of descendants.

One of his correspondents was his mother, Tabitha Glover, nee' Bacon. Apparently Mother Glover was trying to win an army job for one of her other sons or male relatives and things were not going well back in Beverly. So she asked her soldier son if he could ask his friend the commanding general for some help.

He did, Washington responded and Glover wrote back to mother in his precise hand:

October 7, 1776
Dear Mother

Your letter I gave his Excellency, who observed that the 'business' of the army in its confused condition was more than he could possibly attend to, without anything else, but was very sorry to have gentlemen ill-treated or superseded, who had his appointment from him and who had to his satisfaction but all that he at the present can do was to write to Congress or to the Marine committee; which he has done...Mr. Gerry as it is powered in a more view than is his Excellency.

This was not a chatty or gossipy letter from son to mother – it was all business. And the next topic was of interest to all – post war compensation.

Congress, Glover wrote, was considering a plan to create an army of 88 battalions, 15 of which would come from Massachusetts. It would be an army of 64,064 men. When the war was over, they would be compensated with the grants of land and other things including apparel and money.

According to the plan, colonels would receive 500 acres of land; lieutenant colonels, 450; majors, 400; captains, 350; lieutenants and ensigns, 300; non-commissioned officers, 200; and private soldiers, 100 acres of land. The land would be in the state of their origins, for example Glover would be given land in Massachusetts. The private soldiers would also receive a $20 bonus and a new suit of clothes.

Then he had a few choice thoughts on what Congress could have done better:

> Had this been done 12 months ago we should now have had an army who would have been the match for the enemy upon the open field; but at present we dare not meet them there, our army being composed of flying camp, four months levy men and one month militia, who are always uneasy and cannot go through the fatigue and hardships to which soldiers are now exposed.

Like any good frugal New Englander, Glover tried to look after his men and himself as well as he could. They were proud to serve under him and he was just as proud to command them.

Then he told his mother he had some sad news. He describes some of the campaigns, his marches and countermarches as well as the fights at Harlem Heights and Kip's Bay. Finally he had war news he knew his mother would deliver for him. It was not good tidings. He wrote:

Washington's Savior

I lost 2 men in the retreat. Wormwood Trefry of Marblehead and Benjamin Rawden of Lynn.

Your son,
John Glover29

Cabal Country

Not long after the evacuation of Brooklyn, sniping and backbiting against Washington began again among the officers within the army. General Charles Lee, a former British officer and now Washington's second-in-command, freely told anyone who would listen, that Washington needed to be replaced. And he knew who the replacement should be – himself.

Lee was a very odd man. A talented strategist and soldier, he had no patience and he found it impossible to get along with other people, all of who were less capable than he – in his mind anyway. A bachelor, he was continually surrounded by a barking pack – trained hunting dogs.

The other general who felt he was better than the tall Virginian was Washington's own adjutant, Major General Horatio Gates. A large, friendly man, Gates' opinion of himself often outstripped his talent. He was a former major in the British Army during the French and Indian War. The victor at Saratoga, Gates would continually plot until his defeat at Camden, South Carolina in 1780.

---

29 Glover to Tabitha Glover, 10/3/1776, Upham, p. 15.

Washington's Savior

John Glover served under Charles Lee during the remainder of the New York campaign and under Gates at Saratoga and he was never linked to anti-Washington smears.

Evacuating New York

On September 13th, 1776, the Americans began to evacuate New York City. Under Washington's direction, Colonel Glover and his men were responsible for transferring some 500 wounded men, their beds, belongings and any medical equipment from hospitals in New York to American-run ones in New Jersey. They worked from 9 P.M. to sunrise the next day undiscovered and without loss of life. Washington was very pleased with this special service.

At 9 P.M. September 14th, after working more than 36 hours, Glover was ordered to march his brigade to Harlem – a little more than eight miles away – and link up with McDougall's Division. Then, even before he arrived, he was ordered back to where he started, after leaving his baggage train behind and marching without rest or any refreshment.

They turned quickly and made their way back to the Kip's Bay area where General Howe was attempting to land a large force to outflank Washington again.

The lead units of Glover's Brigade ran into a running mass of rabble that had once been a part of the Continental Army.

The Americans under Washington at the approach of the British were panic stricken, broke ranks and fled. No efforts of Washington could bring them into line or stay their flight. A drawn pistol or sword presented to the head was unavailing. They continued their flight until they met Glover and his brigade and their fearless, orderly, soldierly march reassure them. They halted, they fell into the ranks and marched back with him. Washington would not trust men so recently in panic to face the enemy that day, and ordered them to fall back. Glover's men went back with them.[30]

Glover and his men had achieved a mini-miracle by getting those men back into the fight, but he was deeply disappointed that they were kept out of the fray.

By now, Glover's Brigade was exhausted. That night the Colonel wrote; "We fell back about three miles to Dobbs Ferry without food or drink and camped for the night with nothing but the earth underneath us and nothing but Heaven over us." [31]

On September 28th, General Lee ordered his division to move toward White Plains through Dobbs Ferry, so Glover stayed where he was so he could unite with his division.

Several days later, Glover received bad news for the entire brigade. The British had discovered the baggage they had left behind on the march and counter-march, and they celebrated with a huge bonfire in which they burned everything.

---

[30] Upham, p. 12.
[31] Upham, p. 13.

Washington's Savior

In mid-October, Washington held a war council that decided the army should completely abandon Manhattan and fall back on defensive positions at White Plains. They would start the move on the 16th.

On October 18th, Colonel John Glover and his brigade were bivouacked about three miles inland from Long Island Sound on arm land called Pell's Point.

They were to keep an eye on what the Redcoats were doing at Throg's Neck

William Upham wrote that Washington continued to notice Glover, and especially immediately after the withdrawal from Brooklyn. The commander in chief wrote that "his energy and skill displayed by Glover... obtained for him the particular regard and friendship of Washington."[32]

---

[32] Upham, p. 15.

Washington's Savior

Chapter 10

Glover at Pell's Point

Colonel John Glover could not believe what was in front of him. It appeared the entire British Army and Navy was attacking the tiny peninsula where his brigade was camped. Even now soldiers were being rowed ashore and getting into marching formations, less than three miles away.

The Colonel had risen before the sun that day, October 18th, 1776. He took his spyglass and a ceramic mug of coffee with him as he strolled up the rise of the ridge behind which they had camped to stay out of view.

A Forest of Masts

Then he saw the surface of Pelham Bay had suddenly grown a forest of ship's masts, probably more masts than he had seen since the British sailed from Boston. And from those ships came smaller boats, boats filled with those men in the Red Coats again and carrying muskets.

Then he heard rustling in the long uncut hay in which he stood, as Colonel Loammi Baldwin joined him. They said nothing, but both Massachusetts men knew it would a busy day. Baldwin looked at Glover who nodded. Baldwin started towards the camp to get the men moving for the day's activities.

119

As he left, Glover tried to visualize his current predicament.

He knewGeneral Lee, his division commander, was about three miles to the north along Long Island Sound with most of his force. He knew Washington was using the next few days to get the army totally out of Manhattan to previously prepared position in White Plains, to the north in Westchester County.

He assumed that these red coats coming ashore here were the ones that landed on Throg's Neck, three miles to the south several days ago.

Throg's Neck

The British must have used a map that was old and unreliable. They apparently thought Throg's Neck was a peninsula that would lead them into the center of Manhattan Island and perhaps cut off Washington in the city. But it wasn't a peninsula, it was a neck, like Boston neck. It was a marshy island linked to the mainland by a strip of land usually submerged at high tide. Generals Henry Clinton and Lord Cornwallis had a miserable time on Throg's Neck. They spent three days and now they were coming to Pell's Point.

They did not know it, but John Glover would be there to welcome them back to dry land.

Ordering the Battle

Washington's Savior

Glover hurried back down the hill to where Baldwin was forming the regiments. Right now Glover had four under-strength Massachusetts units in his brigade. Glover's 14th Continentals had 179 men ready for duty and, since several of his higher-ranking officers were away on a furlough, the entire regiment would be under the command of Lt. William Courtis of the 1st Company.

The other units were:

1. 13th Massachusetts Continentals, 264 men, Colonel Joseph Read

2. 3rd Massachusetts, 292 men, Colonel William Shepherd

3. 26th Massachusetts, 226 men, Colonel Loammi Baldwin

Glover also had three 12-pound brass field pieces, but he had no time to do anything with them now. He had to move fast so he decided he would leave the guns behind along with the 14th Regiment to form the reserve for the upcoming fight. Glover had the regiments line up in formation, four abreast, Read's regiment leading the way, followed by Shepherd's men and then Baldwin's troops bringing up the rear.

He also sent Brigade Major William Lee to find General Lee and apprise him of situation and to arrange for some reinforcements.

From the beginning, Glover had hoped to contest the landings, but it was much too late for that now – the lobsters were approaching about a mile and half away and coming on quickly. Led by light infantry skirmishers, they were probing to test the strength of their foe.

Four days after the battle, Glover wrote a lengthy letter in which he explained his strategy and provided a running account of the struggle. It is the only original document describing what happened that day.

In the report, Glover made no bones about his lack of experience in fighting a set piece such as Pell's Point. He wrote:

> I would have given a thousand worlds to have General Lee, or some other experienced officer present, to direct me or at least to approve what I had done. I could see none, they all being three miles from me, and the action came on and so sudden it was out of me.[33]

He need not have worried. Military analysts would later say a professionally trained career officer could not have done better.

Glover had started by anchoring Colonel Read's left flank to 'Glover's Rock,' a huge granite outcropping that today still exists and still bears the name of the Colonel from Marblehead. Today, the rock is located in the modern day town of Mt. Vernon, N.Y. From the great rock, Read spread the rest of the regiment across the road and behind the stonewall. Some distance behind that line was Colonel Shepherd's regiment, following the contours of the wall. Finally Baldwin's regiment was in a similar position behind Shepherd.

---

[33] Upham, p.15.

Washington's Savior

Now mounted on horseback, so his men could see and hopefully hear him, Glover led his 40-man guard against the line of British skirmishers and fought them to a standstill. Then the Americans withdrew towards Read's line as more Redcoats came up and added pressure to the attacks.

When the British got within the range of a musket shot, Read's men stood up and poured a withering fire into the red ranks. The surprised British took it, wavered, and fired a volley of their own and then took a defensive position.

Glover continues the account in his letter of October 22th, 1776:

> We exchanged seven rounds at this point, retreated and then formed in the rear of Col. Shepherd and to his left; and then they shouted and pushed on until they reached Col. Shepherd, posted behind a fine double stonewall...he rose up and fired by grand division, by which he kept up a constant fire and maintained post until he exchanged 17 rounds and forced them back several times.[34]

A Withering Volley

Now this time, the British thought they really had the Americans on the run. As Glover and his men fell back on the final American line, more and more British soldiers pursued them and were gaining ground on the rebels. All of a sudden Baldwin's line rose up and fired an unexpected and devastating volley into the charging mass of British infantrymen. The

---

[34] Upham, p.15.

unsuspecting men took the awful fire. The few officers who lived through it now ordered the survivors to fall back to a defensive position.

The surprised lobsters-backs settled in defensively as they tried to gauge the size and identity of their tenacious foe. Next, the British cannons began to bombard the American lines, drawing the fire of the trio of American guns that Glover had left on the slope of the hill in order to command the field. The cool air of this fall afternoon was soon filled with the sharp sounds of an artillery duel.

For hours now, Glover had been looking for help in the form of General Lee, but no troops could be found by lookouts in any direction. In any event, Colonel Glover was now looking for a way out before he was overwhelmed. He had held the British off for hours and the day was growing short and still no sign of help. He broke things off slowly, almost man by man, all the while maintaining artillery fire. But the British showed no inclination to continue and they did not follow him.

Glover conceded the field to the British, and meanwhile continued to withdraw until his brigade reached Dobbs Ferry, which was several miles away. The British, counting their dead and tending to their wounded, camped where Glover's brigade pitched their tents the night before. They thought they had engaged a much larger force than a severely under-sized American brigade.

A tired John Glover sat in his tent that night, trying to write a report on what happened at Pell's Point.   He later wrote to his mother, Tabitha in Marblehead, that the brigade had suffered eight men killed, and thirteen wounded, one whom was Col. Shepherd, who Glover called 'a very brave man."

The British at Pell's Point were still trying to figure out what happened and who they had encountered.   During the day, they unloaded about 4,000 troops and many of them were fed directly into the battle.   Casualty estimates for General Howe's army ranged from 400 to 800 men.   Most experts feel that the lower number is more accurate.

A Special Notice . . . and Pork and Flour

The very next day, General Lee sought out Colonel Glover.   Glover did not know his new superior officer very well yet, the eccentric general having just returned from victories at Charleston, South Carolina.   Glover knew Lee did not suffer fools easily, and usually had something he wanted whenever he sought out a certain officer. So Glover assumed Lee wanted something – and he did.

Lee said during the evacuation the Americans had left some 200 barrels of flour and pork behind in Eastchester.   Now the British controlled the village, but Lee wondered if Glover would like to recover the food to replace other lost rations.

Glover told Lee he would give it try.   He

later wrote about this incident in another letter to the folks at home. "I sent out and pressed 15 wagons, and at night turned out the whole brigade, and went down so nigh here the enemy we've heard the music and talk, and we brought out the whole." [35]

Yet another success for John Glover.

And more would follow. On the following Wednesday, Glover sent out a scouting party that ran into a larger group of mounted Hessians. The outnumbered Americans never hesitated and attacked the German forces, killed twelve, captured three and drove the rest away.

The American high command certainly appreciated what Glover and his 'web-footed infantry' had recently done. On October 19, 1776, Lee's General order for the day included the following:

> General Lee returns his warmest thanks to Colonel Glover and on the brigade under his command, not only for their gallant behavior yesterday but for their prudent, cool, orderly and soldier-like conduct in all respects. He assures these brave men that he shall omit no opportunity of showing his gratitude.[36]

Washington added his gratitude to Glover in a section of his general orders two days later:

> The hurried situation of the Gen. the last two days have prevented him from paying him attention to Colonel Glover and the officers and soldiers were with him on a skirmish on Friday last that their

[35] Upham, p. 15
[36] Ibid.

merit and good behavior deserved.

The Virginian added that Glover's rear guard action was vital to the successful withdrawal of the entire Continental Army to safety in Westchester County. He himself was occupied with that duty, as was General Lee and most of the other members of his staff.

Washington praised Glover for taking the initiative to engage the invaders immediately rather than letting them come ashore and move inland and possibly disrupt the Continentals as they made their way to safety in White Plains. Washington held up Glover and the 14th Regiment as good examples of how he hoped all units would respond to similar challenges.[37]

History's Judgment

Now to the question of why the Battle of Pell's Point is often ignored and almost forgotten by most historians. There are several reasons. First of all, in his general orders of October 21st, 1776, while lauding Glover and his men, Washington called that engagement a 'skirmish,' and no doubt a skirmish it will remain. No one questioned it when he designated it as such; his decision was final. And rarely are skirmishes studied in depth and honored by historians. Never mind that a failure by Glover at Pell's Point could put Howe once again in a position to roll up Washington and the Revolution and send both to

---

[37] Ibid.

the prison hulks.

Second, in the tradition of the 18th century military, a real battle involved a strategic engagement of near epic proportions. Also, for a battle to be considered a victory, winning army had to retain the field. Glover not only had a small force, but he left the field to the British, giving them the "victory". And it was very unusual for a mere "colonel" to win such a victory.

Chapter 11

Racing to the Delaware

By the middle of November, the Continental Army had been thrown out of New York lock, stock, and barrel by the British.

They had been beaten, battered, and bruised in New York almost continuously since the fighting began in late August of 1776.

Now the entire Continental Army had all of its feet on the ground in one state – New Jersey. But in spite of this defeat, giving up was the last thing George Washington had on his mind.

In addition to losing New York, Washington had also done something very unmilitary – he divided his meager army into three pieces and sent them off into the New Jersey hinterlands.

This division of forces violated one of the key tenets of military theory, but in 1776 it was a relief that Washington could do it. This way the British had to chase three different forces across New Jersey, the units were smaller, easier to command, and control, and much more difficult to find. And as long as one part of the army survived, so did the Revolution.

Major General Nathanael Greene commanded the largest division – 6,000 men.

Washington's Savior

Washington was with Greene, as usual. Washington had been forced to watch the surrender of his garrisons at Forts Lee and Washington on the New Jersey and New York sides of the river respectively. By November 10th, Greene and his men were in Newark, and Henry Knox and his artillery joined them on the 22nd, and they headed south. Howe, who had landed on the New Jersey Palisades, picked up the chase and followed the Continentals, as a foot race across the narrow state of New Jersey began.

Greene's force quick-stepped to New Brunswick and destroyed a bridge over the Raritan River, but even that did not stop the hard-charging Lord Cornwallis, who was leading Howe's troops. By December 3rd, 1776, the Continental's were fast-approaching the Delaware River several miles to the north of the village of Trenton. Washington had great hopes for the river. As long as it didn't freeze, the river should give the Army breathing room and a chance to rest.

But the Americans had a surprise for the British – there would be no boats for Lord Cornwallis; the American quartermasters had taken them all. The British did not know it, but for the last two weeks Washington's quartermasters had been scouring the New Jersey bank of the Delaware River to find boats to use when Washington's troops arrived. By the time the British got to Trenton there were no boats within thirty miles in both directions.

The Delaware

Greene arrived on the afternoon of December 3rd and the boats were ready. Within hours, the crossing had begun. They ferried the men, the camp followers and women, the horses, the tents, the stores, the guns, everything had to go.

It took five days, working around the clock, to get the army into Pennsylvania. Rough water and cold reduced the number of boats available. Many of the crews were unfamiliar with rowing and had to be replaced or given rest frequently. Men prayed that Glover and his men would show up.

Washington must have wished the 14th Massachusetts were with him now. They were good men to have around. Cornwallis, however, still hadn't shown up and that made certainly the crossing easier.

Finally, the last American boat was pulled onto the Pennsylvania shore. Almost simultaneously, the British infantry reached the New Jersey side of the river in a rush to the bank to see what was going on. They fired several salvos across the water at the Americans landing, but the river was too wide at that point for the fire to hit them. That damned Washington had escaped from Howe once again.

Second Division

The second division of about 4,000 men,

was actually the rearguard of the army, and was under the command of Major General Charles Lee. Among the units under his command were the web-footed warriors from Marblehead.

By now, Lee had begun to despise Washington. An experienced officer with years of service in the British army, he truly believed he deserved Washington's job. He would tell anyone who would listen that Washington was not qualified to command a "corporal's guard."

After crossing the Hudson further north beyond New York City, Lee and his men languished for several weeks at the old army camp at Peekskill.

Almost daily, messages and orders from Washington arrived and were then quickly read and forgotten by Lee. Finally, after waiting and waiting as long as he could, Lee gave the order to break camp on November 30th.

Third Division

The third of the rebel armies or detachments moving through New Jersey was actually a contingent of soldiers from Fort Ticonderoga being reassigned to the Continental Army. Major General Horatio Gates, Washington's former adjutant and another secret supplicant for the top job, commanded the 600 men.

Gates, however, was not particularly popular with his troops. Most of his men called him 'granny' because he reminded them of a fussy old woman.

Glover and Lee

Lee had been quick to understand the value and the competency of Glover and his brigade. They had recaptured the missing pork and flour and Lee was pleased with the Hessians whom Glover's men unhorsed in their recent battle when mounted men from Marblehead routed a group of professional Hessian cavalrymen.

They soon showed they could do more.

On October 25th, Lee's division guarded the rear of the army as it moved from Kingsbridge, on the northern end of Manhattan Island, to White Plains. Glover was given responsibility of moving all the military baggage and stores from his division safely to the new lines. It was a lot of extra work for the brigade but they got the entire baggage train of more than 100 wagons to the military lines in Westchester County.

Three days later, Glover's Brigade was involved in rear guard action at the Battle of White Plains. They stood solidly on the defense long enough to allow the bulk of the army to retreat safely to New Jersey while they fought at several crossroads to keep the main thoroughfare open.

Breakfast at the Tavern

Lee moved his division slowly through the New Jersey hill country in early December. They were still moving west and Glover and John Sullivan, now Lee's deputy, both worried about Washington and they hoped they would join him soon.

On December 10th, they were just a few miles south of Morristown near the tiny village of Basking Ridge, when he told his officers he would spend the night at a country inn, White's Tavern. Lee quickly gathered his dogs and left.

Early the next morning, Lee was breakfasting with Captain James Wilkinson,[38] General Gates' aide. The younger man looked up and saw green-coated British cavalry approaching quickly from the nearby woods. Lee was still in his dressing gown and he made no effort to escape. Wilkinson, however, slipped out a back door and ran to his horse and rode off as fast as he could to tell Gates and Sullivan what had happened.

Sullivan was flabbergasted by the incident, wondering aloud whether Lee had planned the

---

[38] James Wilkinson was probably the **second most shadowy** figure in early American history. He always seemed to show up as an aide to an anti-heroic character like Gates and somehow got away scot-free. He seemed to have no concept of law or morality. Twice he was thrown out of United States Army, yet in 1799 became the senior officer of the same organization even though it was common knowledge that he was also a paid agent of the King of Spain. Wilkinson was probably the only person who knew the scope of the treachery of Aaron Burr, the former Vice President of the United States and the **MOST shadowy figure** in early American history. In 1807, Burr was tried for treason and acquitted by a jury in New Orleans. Wilkinson died in 1825.

capture himself.[39]   But Sullivan did know he would waste neither time nor lives on trying to rescue Charles Lee. Within hours, Lee's division was moving south toward the Delaware River to rendezvous with Washington – and without Charles Lee.

---

[39] Lee was captured by Lt. Col. Banastre Tarleton, who later in the war would be known as "the butcher of the south" due to the brutality of his actions against citizens and soldiers. It is unlikely that Lee planned his capture with the British. In fact, they treated him more like a rebel than an honorable foe. Most of his time was spent in solitary confinement in a military jail in Brunswick, N.J., until he was exchanged about a year later.

Chapter 12

The American Crisis

He had done it before. But could he do it again? There were doubts. In 1775, Thomas Paine had proven that the pen is a mightier than the sword.

Paine had done it with his pamphlet called simply *Common Sense.* This slim 42-page booklet gave many of the people in those thirteen soon-to-be united colonies the reasons and the rationale for revolting against the British. Taken in perspective, it was a remarkable document and it made Paine a rich man.

The political and the intellectual rebels of the 18th century seemed to be very concerned with the literary preservation of their thoughts, ideas and principles. The Continental Congresses were no different. They had their Olive Branch Petition, the Declaration of Independence, and other documents that were recording history as it was being made.

In any event, Paine has tried it again with a new booklet. This one was known simply as *The American Crisis.*

Washington picked up the pamphlet and began to read. The first line caught his eye – *"These are the times that try men's souls".* He liked what he read.

On December 23rd, 1776, several hundred

pamphlets were distributed throughout the army so officers could read it to the troops huddled around fires burning along the Delaware River.

Washington wanted his men to know what they were fighting for. And he hoped many would re-enlist in the army before January 1st.

The officers read:

THESE are times that try men's souls. The summer soldier and the sunshine patriot will, in this crisis, shrink from the service of their country; but he that stands by it now, deserves the love and thanks of man and woman. Tyranny, like hell, is not easily conquered; yet we have this consolation with us, that the harder the conflict, the more glorious the triumph. What we obtain too cheap, we esteem too lightly: it is dearness only that gives everything its value. Heaven knows how to put a proper price upon its goods; and it would be strange indeed if so celestial an article as FREEDOM should not be highly rated. Britain, with an army to enforce her tyranny, has declared that she has a right (not only to TAX) but "to BIND us in ALL CASES WHATSOEVER" and if being bound in that manner, is not slavery, then is there not such a thing as slavery upon earth. Even the expression is impious; for so unlimited a power can belong only to God.

Whether the independence of the continent was declared too soon, or delayed too long, I will not now enter into as an argument; my own simple opinion is, that had it been eight months earlier, it

Washington's Savior

would have been much better. We did not make proper use of last winter, neither could we, while we were in a dependent state. However, the fault, if it were one, was all our own; we have none to blame but ourselves. But no great deal is lost yet. All that Howe has been doing for this month past is rather a ravage than a conquest, which the spirit of the Jerseys, a year ago, would have quickly repulsed, and which time and a little resolution will soon recover.

Thomas Paine came from England in 1774, on the recommendation of Benjamin Franklin. He was a 37-year-old failure at everything. But somehow he more than any other man, was able to codify the feeling of the American Revolution and put it down on paper for everyone to share.

He worked for a printer as a writer and publicist, but it was his pamphlets *Common Sense* and *The American Crisis* that were working instruments that helped to inspire the lives of the Revolutionaries during the long years of its duration. Paine served in the Continental Army for a while, but later worked for the Continental Congress and the Pennsylvania Assembly.

He moved to France in 1787. There he played a prominent role in the propagation of the French Revolution of 1789, and was well known throughout the country as a writer and propagandist for the Revolutionary movement. Paine died in 1809 in poverty. He is considered to be one of the nation's Founding Fathers. Here is the last paragraph Paine wrote in *The American Crisis*:

Washington's Savior

Thank God that I fear not. I see no real cause for fear. I know our situation well, and can see the way out of it. While our army was collected, Howe dared not risk a battle; and it is no credit to him that he decamped from the White Plains, and waited a mean opportunity to ravage the defenseless Jerseys but it is great credit to that, with a handful of men, we sustained an dearly retreat for near an hundred miles, brought off our ammunition, all our field pieces, the greatest part of our stores, and had four rivers to pass. None can say that our retreat was precipitate, for we were near three weeks in performing it, that the country might have time to come in. Twice we marched back to meet the enemy, and remained out till dark. The sign of fear was not seen in our camp, and had not some of the cowardly and disaffected inhabitants spread false alarms through the country, the Jerseys had never been ravaged. Once more we are again collected and collecting; our new army at both ends of the continent is recruiting fast, and we shall be able to open the next campaign with sixty thousand men, well armed and clothed. This is our situation, and who will may know it. By perseverance and fortitude we have the prospect of a glorious issue; by cowardice and submission, the sad choice of a variety of evils — a ravaged country — a depopulated city — habitations without safety, and slavery without hope — our homes turned into barracks and bawdy-houses for Hessians, and a future race to provide for, whose fathers we shall doubt of. Look on this picture and weep over it! And if there yet remains one thoughtless wretch

139

Washington's Savior

who believes it not, let him suffer it unlamented.

Well-positioned and well-protected by nature, Marblehead harbor served as a safe haven for Glover's navy and the fleet of privateers that he helped recruit to drive the British from Boston. *Photo by Trevor Brayall.*

In this quaint harbor, in 1775, John Glover prepared his schooner *Hannah* for war. *Photo by Trevor Brayall.*

The John Glover House in Marblehead, Massachusetts. Today it is a private residence. *Photo by Trevor Brayall.*

This plaque commemorates John Glover for his contributions to the revolution and today is attached to the outside of his house in Marblehead. *Photo by Trevor Brayall.*

For years, this statue of John Glover has stood watch over the approaches to Boston along that city's Commonwealth Avenue. The inscription on the statue reads "John Glover....a soldier of the Revolution."

Emmanuel Leutze's famous painting showing Washington crossing the Delaware provides an idealistic view of the evening. In reality, the men from Marblehead endured terrible cold and stinging frozen shards of sleet in the air as they brought the Continentals back to New Jersey. The rowers also had to dodge huge chunks of ice that nearly clogged the waterway; no one could stand in the boats let alone strike any heroic poses and still remain dry enough to take part in the upcoming struggle.

John Glover was a fighting general.

Chapter 13

Crossing the Delaware

Henry Knox had noted a change in General Washington as the reunited yet disillusioned Continental Army marched across New Jersey. He often seemed preoccupied, overly tired, and uncharacteristically upset.

Knox knew the General had received a number of new messages from Congress and he wondered if that was not the problem.

In fact, one such message did help brighten George Washington's overall outlook. The December 12th message notified him Congress was retiring to the safety of Baltimore and that Washington was to assume all of their powers – and to wield his own – until further notice. He literally was in charge of everything.

What Washington wanted, however, was his army back together and all in one place. Generals Lee and Gates continued to ignore his request to centralize forces, and he knew if the Delaware ever froze, Howe and Cornwallis would be on him in an instant, and there would be no escape this time. He continued to pray for warm weather.

Granny Comes to Camp

Washington's Savior

In mid-December, "Granny" Gates finally arrived at the army's main camp in the village of Morrisville after a long march from Ticonderoga. But Gates seemed contrary, negative, out of sorts, and wanted no movement taken by the army without General Lee's concurrence. He grimaced visibly when told what had happen to Lee. Many other members of the officer corps began to wonder just exactly who Gates was loyal to.

Horatio Gates was not an incompetent soldier. The son of the housekeeper to the Duke of Bolton's mistress, he was able to purchase a commission as a subaltern lieutenant in a British infantry regiment. He eventually rose to the rank of major and served in wars in both Europe and North America.

When he settled in North America, he became neighbor and friend to a Virginia planter named George Washington.

The lucky recipient of a major general's commission in the Continental Army, he had begun to believe he deserved even more, based largely on Washington's performance in the New York campaign fiasco. Now he was just waiting for his moment to come.

Fife and Drums but no General Lee

On December 20th, Washington heard the faint sounds of approaching fifes and drums. It could only be Lee and now he could re-unite the army and get back to the business of revolution.

It was Lee's division, but Lee was nowhere

to be seen. General John Sullivan of New Hampshire, who Washington was very glad to see, was leading the formation. Washington's old friend told him the story of Lee's capture at the tavern in Basking Ridge. The Virginian was astonished by the story and wondered how a man as intelligent as Lee could be so careless and stupid at the same time. He could manage no great sympathy for the man.

The General must have smiled, however, when he saw the 14th Massachusetts and the rest of the Second Massachusetts Brigade march into camp under the sharp eye of a well-mounted Colonel John Glover.

The equestrian colonel was glad to see Washington. He did not miss Charles Lee.

A Plan for Victory

George Washington had a plan to revive the Continental Army and to refresh the Revolution. But he had to use his army now, before it disintegrated, which it would do January 1st when many of the enlistments in the Continental Army expired. Washington was afraid there would be little army left at the end of that day.

In the past several weeks, Knox had noticed Washington fiddling with two small pieces of paper covered with scrawled scribbling. At one time Knox was able to read the writing clearly. They were two small, simple words, strong and straightforward – *victory* or *death* – and they made his blood run cold.

Victory or Death

On Christmas Eve, Washington presented his plan to his generals and commanders.

It called for the tiny army to move on Trenton as night fell on Christmas Day and attack the Hessian garrison there before daybreak. He was sure the Hessians would be a bit groggy at that time due to their holiday celebrations.

According to the details of the plan, the veteran American General Israel Putnam, would cross the river from Philadelphia and feint towards British in Burlington, N.J.

Two smaller units would cross to the south of Trenton, but the main army under Washington would cross the river at McConkey's Ferry, about eight miles north of the small riverside settlement. Then Nathanael Greene would take his division along with Pennington Sullivan would direct his men along the River Road. The two roads would merge again in Trenton.

The watchword for the attack would be "liberty or death."

Washington then named Colonel Henry Knox to command at the loading site[40] and he would be in overall command of the crossing. Then he asked for volunteers to handle the boats.

According to legend, John Glover rose and

---

[40] This appointment would not have pleased Glover. He and Knox had at times had a contentious relationship, mainly because the former Boston bookseller often outranked Glover, who was nearly 20 years his senior. The pair rarely saw eye-to-eye on anything, and Glover often used his sharp tongue to remind Knox of his girth and weight.

stood as tall as his frame would allow and said loudly that his men from Marblehead would take the army across the river and back again.

Other accounts recall a private meeting, where Glover bluntly told Washington that he was asking the impossible. But whatever the reality, Glover's Brigade manned the boats.

Glover's Men did not Work Alone

Glover's Marbleheaders were one of three organizations that did the boat work, but they all looked to Glover and his men for leadership and guidance.

The second group consisted of Delaware River boatmen from various other regiments, who volunteered together in a river they knew well. The third group, were small boat veterans from other parts of the new country willing to lend their arms and backs to the crossing.

Washington took no vote at this meeting, these were orders his troops would follow and not question the operation. This was an order and not a plan. Democracy would exist in his army's high command only at his discretion.

As the officers left to tell their men, they were also given copies of reading material for all – freshly printed copies of Tom Paine's new work. *The American Crisis.*

Misbehaving Granny

Horatio Gates was acting up again. He wanted Lee and he wanted no part of

Washington's Savior

Washington's latest plan for disaster. It got even worse when Washington offered him overall command of the operation in Lee's absence. Instead of accepting, Gates feigned sickness. He then sought permission to seek medical treatment in nearby Philadelphia. Washington agreed and Granny left right away.

Gates went to Philadelphia but he sought no medical treatment for his convenient yet undiagnosed illness. He would wait at Congress and would be ready to take over command when the news arrived about the defeat at Trenton. But Congress, he discovered, was in Baltimore. He turned his horse south.

The Army Gets Ready

All Christmas Day, Washington's men were very busy preparing for their return to New Jersey. Each man had to bring three days worth of food with them, so the cook fires burned early. They cleaned their guns, checked and rechecked their powder and shot, and tried to keep their clothes as dry as possible. They oiled their bayonets so they wouldn't rust – they might need them.

Some finished reading Paine's latest pamphlet, and then those who would, among those who could, read the pamphlet to those who couldn't. Many more slept or took catnaps to prepare for the upcoming ordeal.

By five P.M., bloody tracks in the snow led to McConkey's Tavern and ferry, showing with scarlet alacrity what snow did to marching bare feet. But march they did and by the appointed hour, 2900 men were waiting to cross.

Durham Boats

Glover and his men took stock of the boats collected this time by the army quartermasters. Among the craft were a large number of Durham boats. These river rowboats – built by the Durham mining company – were much larger than the normal boats and were used to ship ore to Philadelphia for refining.

Some were up to sixty feet long and four feet wide, though most were twenty to forty feet long. They were extremely sturdy and seaworthy and Glover thought they would certainly carry more men at one time than ordinary boats and therefore save time.

The boats were in the water by 5 P.M., but it took sometime before the crews were ready to go. Washington watched with growing impatience.

First boats in the water

Among the first groups to present themselves for passage was a brigade from the Virginia line commanded by one of Washington's neighbors on the Potomac, General Adam Stephen. His job was to use his men to form a perimeter around the beachhead to protect the boats as they landed. They would take into custody any civilians who might find such information useful to the Hessians.

The Problems Multiply

Although Henry Knox was the commanding officer at the loading point, his mind seemed to be somewhere else. And it was. He was focusing on how he would transport the fourteen field pieces Washington had ordered. The Durham boats would not work, nor would most of the other craft they had at the shore.

John Glover worked with his fellow Bay Stater to find a solution and a quick one. They concluded the large ferry boats that carried horse-drawn carriages and wagons during more peaceful times, would be perfect conveyances for the cannon and other equipment.

Next, the horses became a problem. They refused to get into the Durham boats, and there were no fords close by that they could use to walk them across the waterway, someone suggested they use the big ferries for the animals they tried it and it worked.

Another problem was visibility. This night was very dark, and the weather would not provide a lot of help at the crossing. Boats were bumping others and crashing into the ice flows, which were getting thicker and more numerous as time went by.

Washington Crosses

At 2 A.M., Glover held back a returning boat manned by two of his best watermen. Captain William Blackler and Private John

Washington's Savior

Russell, both of Marblehead. Glover beckoned to a grim faced Washington and suggested he take this boat over to New Jersey. When that particular Durham boat reached the shore again, it contained, according to legend, an impressive list of American historical figures, including George Washington and his aide Major Alexander Hamilton, Henry Knox, and a young lieutenant and future president of the United States named James Monroe.

Meanwhile, seconds passed and turned into minutes, minutes passed and turned into hours, and the dawn came even closer for the frustrated Washington. He had planned this operation to the minute and he knew he had to allow four hours to march to Trenton and he already should have been on the road. He asked Glover how much longer he needed. Glover told him he would let him know.

At 4 A.M., he sent a note over to the General, who was anxiously pacing the riverbank. The last boats were in the water now, he wrote. He was about done.

On the shore, Washington was out of sorts. The timing of his plan was crucial and he wanted his army to attack the Hessians at Trenton before sunrise, which was about two hours away. They would never keep that schedule now because the crossing took longer than he had expected. Washington knew his army would be in trouble if they lost and the Hessian commander knew the Continentals were coming. He could request reinforcements from the string of posts the British established throughout New Jersey at places like

Princeton, Bordentown, Mt. Holly, and Brunswick.

Washington also got other news. The two other contingents suppose to cross the Delaware failed in their efforts because of ice and returned to camp. Washington would have no reinforcements. And, he learned later, General Putnam never left Philadelphia to do his role in the operation.

In spite of these failures, the two divisions were formed and within the hour they were marching on Trenton. General Nathanael Greene, accompanied, of course, by Washington, was marching on the Pennington Road, while John Sullivan was leading Lee's division, including John Glover's very tired brigade, on the River Road. All told Washington was bringing about 2,900 men to fight 1,900 Hessians.

Paid Soldiers for Britain

Because England did not have a large standing army, George III hired mercenary troops from the German principality of Hesse-Cassell – hence called Hessians – to do much of the fighting. These German combatants, highly trained and disciplined, were often called the best foot soldiers in the world. During the many skirmishes in the battle for New York, soldiers from the Knyphausen division of Hessians were particularly cruel to American forces, repeatedly assaulting them with a strange and horrible weapon – the bayonet.

Throughout the war, American soldiers

were uncommonly brutal to any Hessians who were captured in retribution. After the war, however, thousands of Hessians stayed in the United States and became strong and loyal citizens of the new nation.

The Battle of Trenton

The story of the Battle of Trenton is well told and better written elsewhere, so I'll repeat just the essentials here. Although the army arrived at 8 A.M. in Trenton, the Americans had not lost the element of surprise. The Greene and Sullivan divisions united and were waiting to greet the Hessians as they were roused from their post-holiday slumber in their barracks.

Among those who came out was Colonel Johan Rall – through the smoke of Henry Knox's cannon fire, he tried to form a ragged battle line with his men. He even got several of his German cannon on the line and ready to defend. but to no avail. The only thanks he got for this was a musket ball in his abdomen. The wound was mortal; he died later that afternoon.

Ironically, folded inside of one of Rall's uniform pockets was a note he received from a Tory telling him that Washington was going to try to attack his force on Christmas Day. He never opened it.

A Substantial Skirmish

Little more than a skirmish, Trenton was

nevertheless a great victory for the Americans. Washington's victory was of little military significance, but it provided great fodder for the propagandists. At the cost of no dead and two wounded, he captured almost 900 prisoners; a number of cannon, powder, shot and muskets; blankets; shoes; everything his army needed.

As Washington tried to process the enormity of what he and his men had done that day, he was awed. He wandered over the field, going from group to group, just thanking them for doing such a wonderful job. He told them they had saved the Revolution.

All the while, Washington was looking for Colonel John Glover. He finally found him by the banks of the Delaware, where he was talking to another of the General's curmudgeons, New Hampshire General John Stark. Washington greeted both men, thanked them for their brave work, and told Glover he should prepare to row again.

Washington did not wait in Trenton to rest his men. He pushed them and he prodded them to get back across the river before Cornwallis or someone else found out about the attack and marched on Trenton for countermeasures against the Americans. As he commanded, the army walked in good order back the eight miles to the boats. Then Glover and his men – having fought and marched like the others – picked up their oars and safeguarded the army once again.

Once back in his lines, Washington seemed like a new man. His confidence was high, he was proud of his men, and now he had won his first battle. His relationship with Congress changed as well – he was more forceful, more in-charge, and the congressmen remembered that while they left for Baltimore and safety, Washington had remained in the field and, in one very dark hour, had saved the Army, the Revolution and the United States of America.

One thing Washington was determined to do was reward his men and officers. He quickly wrote out a list and told the Congress he wanted the men on it promoted as soon as possible. Near the top of the list for brigadier general was the name of John Glover.

Chapter 15

The End of the 14th

It must have been a shock to the psyche of the rest of the Continental Army when they saw just what units were leaving the force now the enlistments had expired for the men on January 1ˢᵗ, 1777.

The regulars of the Continental Line surely expected some of the militia regiments would go; they were nowhere near professional in their skills. The army could always count on having a few of those regiments leaving camp as new ones were coming in.

Actually, Washington and his triumph at Trenton had caused a majority of the army to re-enlist and he was planning a per-soldier bonus that he would pay out of his own pocket if it would encourage more men to stay. Even that would not keep them all, he knew.

But no one, no one who knew the Continental Army ever would have thought the Marbleheaders would be among the regiments to go.

For God's sake, these were Glover's men. The damn men from Marblehead who saved the army over and over again in the last six months. The web-footed warriors. And Glover was gone too.

Washington hoped the victory at Trenton

154

would encourage units on the fence about leaving to either stay en masse or in groups that each could at least retain an identity.

The 14th Massachusetts had answered every call from Washington, had followed every order and had faced every foe that had come forward since the very day they had crossed paths at the American camp in Cambridge. And while their most recent act of heroism was considered by many their most impressive, the fact that they were able to transport the army across the Delaware, and not once but twice, made that essential victory at Trenton a reality

But Washington knew what was coming. He and Glover had discussed the matter before and he knew where the little colonel stood and why.

As David Hackett Fischer wrote, in his *Washington's Crossing:*

> Some of his best regiments seemed determined to depart. One of them was a Glover's Marblehead mariners, who wanted to go home for a special reason. Many men planned to leave the army so they could fight at sea[41].

The End of the 14th

The men from Marblehead had heard about the money to be made in privateering – which was being made by their friends and relatives back home. As Glover no doubt told Washington, his men were watermen who were more at home on

---

[41] Fischer, David Hackett, *Washington's Crossing, p. 27.*

the deck of a ship than on dry land. They had proven they could fight at Pell's Point and at White Plains, but if they were going to be used as boatmen they might as well make some money.

It appeared like the entire regiment was in favor of this change. When Glover's adjutant and Brigade Major William Lee tried to reconstitute a regiment combining veterans with new soldiers with new officers and men, he could only interest nine officers to fill his 37 vacancies.[42]

When Glover and his men left the camp, the 14th Massachusetts Continental Regiment was disbanded, their flags and banners furled forever and the regiment went out of existence.

The Marblehead mariners, the web-footed warriors, were walking home to Massachusetts.

Warrior at Home

Looking through old papers and letters, it is difficult to determine exactly how Glover felt about this. There's little doubt that he wanted to be at home – at least for a while. For nearly two years of war, John Glover had been away from his home – but so have many other men. He was tired, but so were many other men.

That was not all. His wife was sick, and he still had younger children – eight under the age of 15 – at home. His business was in shambles and he felt an obligation to the family to put it back in shape. He was also certain that he would either own or captain a privateer which could change is entire life. One good prize rightly captured could

[42] Sanborn p. 26.

enrich a man forever.

Another thought may have crossed his mind. His regiment had been raised to protect their home. Now the British were gone and they might or might not be back. Let someone else fight the British, we have already driven them away. Let New Jersey men fight for New Jersey rights and freedoms like we did in Massachusetts.

From all appearances, he enjoyed being at home for a while. Until February 21st, 1777. On that day he became a Brigadier General.

A Star Falls on Glover

Congress finally realized it had to provide for Washington's men and they did so, giving him every new general he wanted. John Glover apparently was not excited when he heard the news. He tried, somehow through Washington, to decline the honor, but the General would not hear of it.

In a letter to Glover written on April 25th, 1777, Washington told him he would not have included him on the promotions list if he was not expected to serve. Now, after that mild rebuke, Glover may have figured he would be home scot free, but instead he ran full-force into the power of Washingtonian psychology.

"Diffidence as an officer is a good mark," wrote the commanding general "because he always endeavors to bring himself up to what he conceives to be the full line of his duty."

Now the General flattered Glover with

something he usually had withheld before – praise. "But I think I may tell you without flattery, that I know of *no man better qualified than you to conduct a brigade.*[43] You have activity and industry; and as you very well know the duty of colonel, you know to exact that duty from others."

Reading those words written in Washington's own steady hand, Glover knew it would be very hard to turn him down. The next paragraphs made it impossible:

> I have with great concern observed the almost universal listlessness that prevails, throughout the continent; and I believe that nothing has contributed to it more than the resignation of officers who stepped early forward and led the onto the great cause; in which we are embarked too deeply now to look back, or to hope for any other terms than we gain by the sword. Is any resistance to be expected from the people, when deserted by their leaders?

> Our enemies count upon the resignation of every officer of rank at this time, as a distrust of and desertion from the cause, and rejoice accordingly. When you consider these matters, I hope you will not think of private inconvenience, but that you will come with all expedition, to the command that has been assigned to you. As I fully depend upon seeing you, I shall *not mention anything that has passed between us on this subject to the Congress.*[44]

I am, sir, your most humble servant,

Geo. Washington[45]

---

[43] Author's italics.
[44] Author's italics.
[45] Washington to Glover, 4/25/1777, Upham, p. 21.

A Master of Psychology

Over time and out of necessity, George Washington had become a master psychologist, able to wrap grown men around his little finger, just as he did here with Glover. He praised the man from Marblehead. Then he took away all of his arguments with his own rhetoric. Finally, he promised anonymity and safety to Glover by not telling congress. This letter itself was a marvelous performance of persuasion.

Shortly after this, the new Brigadier wrote to Washington and told him as soon as he was able to finish a few more things at home, he would return. Even as he was winding up things, eyes began to look toward danger from the British in New York.

Anything But A Fool

The one thing George Washington was not was a fool. He knew what was at stake for himself, for his friends and colleagues in the army and in Congress, and for the country if he did not succeed and lead the Continental Army to victory.

It would not be a pretty picture. King George III had promised that when he vowed to hang the leading traitors in North America.

Washington knew the victory at Boston bought him very, very little. The Continental Army had been victorious because they could wait out the siege of the town longer than the British. Once the food was gone and the Ticonderoga guns had arrived, the British had to go.

Washington went to New York knowing that his army still was not tested, they were truly not veterans yet. He knew when that test came, it would be unexpectedly and more frightening than Washington ever expected. He had no idea how hard it would be.

New York was a much different colony than Massachusetts. The revolutionary spirit was different there. For example on June 23rd, 1775, it seemed like the colonial political leaders were finally having to make a choice. Two VIPs were coming on that day and they would have to choose which one to greet.

The first man was William Tryon, the newly

named royal governor of New York. The second was George Washington, on his way to command Boston. The provincial fathers solved this problem by greeting both at separate receptions.

During the independence debate, New York again showed indecision when initially the delegates could only vote 'present.'

It also seemed that their survival in New York was due more to General Howe than to General Washington. Time and again, Howe would be in position where a single frontal attack – properly coordinated – would defeat the Americans once and for all.

But ghosts, nearly 1,000 ghosts, haunted Howe. Ghosts of his men who marched up the slopes of Breed's Hill that awful day in June. Ghosts dressed in scarlet coats. Ghosts whose bodies were piled like chord wood at the end of a very bloody day. Howe never forgot that day of slaughter and he would refuse to be responsible, for a second.

Washington refused to give up. He couldn't give up, he had risked everything when he joined the revolution; he risked everything everyday he woke up in a uniform. There was no way that he could go back, his fate was sealed already. He would never surrender.

He knew the army was the revolution and the revolution was the army. But one could not exist without the other, and he vowed not to let the army die. When his army could kick this malaise, then his army was back in shape, back in position and when it was back much closer in full strength, Washington would take to the field again more confident and stronger as a general. Never again would his fortune fall so low as it did at the end of 1776.

When he crossed the Delaware in December 1776 to save its life, he knew he would return. And like Douglas MacArthur in the Philippines in 1944, Washington did return to New Jersey in 1777, and he returned to ultimate victory.

But neither Washington nor MacArthur could do it alone. They needed good, quality officers and men who could become the professional soldiers they needed to defeat the enemy. MacArthur got his officers from West Point and his men were mass-produced by the U.S. Army's system of boot and training camps. And they were well-fed and well-paid.

Washington, in turn, got the rawest of the raw, men untrained at anything involved with soldiering. Few knew how to even march. Most were untrained militia, underage boys who had no reason to fight a war.

What the Virginian needed were more pre-made soldiers, more good militia regiments, more men like those of the 14th Massachusetts who now were walking home.

<u>Beyond the Delaware – 1777 - 1800</u>

Trenton was a turning-point battle for both George Washington and John Glover. For Washington, the Delaware victory virtually meant his battlefield education was over. He had passed his exams, he had won his first battle, and he would lose no struggles as badly as New York. He did not win the war's largest battle – Saratoga – but truth be told neither did the man who got all the honors. Benedict Arnold won Saratoga for 'Granny Gates' at Bemis Heights just as surely as Cornwallis destroyed Gates' honor at Camden. But Washington won the last battle, the one that really counted –

Yorktown.

John Glover's military career, so promising at its beginning, would now follow a strange and twisting path that would lead to his retirement in 1782.

Chapter 16

Gates, Arnold and Johnny Burgoyne

Brigadier General John Glover slowly rode his horse into the Continental Army camp at Peekskill, New York, on June 14th, 1777.

He was familiar with the location, his brigade under General Lee having been assigned there last fall before joining the main army on the Delaware. But it felt different this time because he was no longer "just" Colonel Glover – he was the real thing – a real brigadier general. Not bad for a Massachusetts fisherman.

It was a pleasant ride during the spring sunshine and Glover did not act like he was in any kind of a hurry. He was disappointed Washington was not there when he reported, but he was glad to see his old friend – and now his immediate superior officer – Major General Israel Putnam.

'Old Put' outlined the strategic situation for the new general. The Howe brothers remained in New York, and it was expected this force would move up the Hudson, probably as far as Albany, to meet an 8,000-man army coming south via Lake Champlain.

This was the army Benedict Arnold turned

back with his homemade lake navy last fall. During the winter, it was reinforced and got a new commander – Major General John Burgoyne. He was utterly committed to crushing the revolt by linking up with Howe, thus controlling the entire Hudson River and splitting America in half.

But Glover's interest right now was the condition of his brigade and what had happened to it during his absence. Right now it consisted of three regiments from Massachusetts, totaling 865 soldiers. This was about the equivalent of one fully staffed regiment. The regiments were Wigglesworth's, Swift's and Shepherd's. The latter had been with Glover at Pell's Point

Looking around the camp, Glover saw that some conditions had not changed much since the early days in Cambridge. In his absence, many of the soldiers still lived in something approaching squalor in nasty old tents or three faced lean-tos with rotting food and bred rats. Food was still awful and uniforms were complexly irregular. It was as if the army had learned nothing since Boston.

He quickly wrote to the commanding general who was at the army camp in Middle Brook, New Jersey:

> This will inform your Excellency I arrived at this place yesterday. I received General Putnam...Upon inquiring into the state of the troops, I found them in the most shocking condition, without coats, breeches, stockings or shoes; many of them having nothing but a frock and a blanket to cover their nakedness.
>
> Col. Wigglesworth and Col. Swift's regiments are

without tents and there are none to be had. I have ordered for the troop to be ready to march on the shortest notice and had the men had tents to cover them and clothes; I should cross the North River tomorrow. I remain your most immediate, humble servant,

John Glover[46]

The new Brigadier tried several times to cross the Hudson River and join Washington in New Jersey. General Howe, however, caused everyone to be on alert and the Americans had to keep a watchful eye on New York until Howe decided where he was going. That he was going somewhere was not a question – only his destination was. Until he decided to move on Philadelphia or go north to Albany and link up with Burgoyne, Glover and his men were told to remain in their lines.

While Glover waited, he picked up his pen and tried to improve conditions for his men. On June 17th, he wrote to his brother Jonathan – now a member of the General Court in Boston and assigned to the War Committee – and his Marblehead friend and confidant Azor Orne.

The letter was scathing.

He wrote that General Howe and a good portion of his army had left New York in 260 ships, but the ships had sailed into the mists and no one knew where they were going. He found no comfort there, especially if Washington sought combat against Howe like he knew the commanding General would.

---

[46] Glover to Washington.

A defeat would be fatal to us. Should Howe get to Philadelphia, which I have great reason to fear that he will, we have no one to blame but ourselves. Had the people of interest and influence attended to the public interest, we might have army now in the field they would have bid defiance to Howe and his whole force.

But with privateering and stock jobbing (I am sorry to say it) has been the sole object of their attention. Is it not a shamed that America, which boasted over 3 million, should be ravaged or subjected by 18 or 20,000 poltroons?

Glover, in some of his most strident and forceful personal writing of the war, continued:

Rouse my fellow countrymen from your sleepy lethargy and come forth into the field and assist your brethren who are jeopardizing their lives for you, your wives and children as well as for themselves.

Glover obviously believed that more men must be found to fill the ranks of the Continental Army. And right now the army was having trouble doing that.

There was no such thing as a draft or conscription at that point in time, and the various states depended upon the generosity and service of their own citizens who were willing to enlist in militia units or in the professional Continental Army. Glover had an idea that he felt would make perfect sense in helping to fill the ranks:

We must and shall all share the same fate, either freeman or slaves. If there be any among you who plead inability, that ought not to be an excuse; if there be any that are timid and dare not come forth...let them exert themselves by hiring a good able-bodied man and see him well-armed and equipped and equipped, then hand them over to some officer in the Continental service.

Then the Marblehead patriot, sitting in his tent among the human flotsam and jetsam from the colonies that currently made up the Continental Army, used the words that many had perhaps thought about, but few had dare speak aloud or put on paper – military dictator:

I've been a lover of the civil law, and I ever wish to see America governed by it, and I am fully of the opinion that it would be the salvation of this country should martial law to take place, at least for 12 months, and General Washington invested with power to a call forth (any or) all the male inhabitants (if wanted) at 24 hours notice. Then instead of a hearing the disagreeable tidings that our armies are retreating before the enemy, instead we would hear that the enemy has been compelled to leave our land or has been cut to pieces.

I am, sir, your humble obedience servant,

General John Glover [47]

The words must have rushed out of Glover's pen as fast as thought of them. Glover filled the pages quickly. Then the letter went off to his brother and his friend and nothing more was heard of it.

---

[47] John Glover to Jonathan Glover and Azore Orne, 6/17/77, Upham, p 23.

Washington's Savior
The Strategy Unveiled

Although Howe had taken to his ships and disappeared into the Atlantic, the Americans would stay put and watch their defenses until General Howe reappeared.

Glover and his brigade did move a bit to cover some familiar territory when he was ordered to the area of Westchester County which included the spear of ground called Pell's Point. Just after Howe's fleet vanished, on July 23, 1777, John Glover received new orders. They were not what he expected. Instead of joining Washington, he and his brigade were ordered north to join Major General Phillip Schuyler and the makeshift army the general with prestigious Dutch pedigree was gathering to meet the mighty onslaught of John Burgoyne.

The Continental Armies

In reality, there were three Continental Armies that served the revolution and represented the Second Continental Congress. The first was the main army under Washington that seemed to be defending the Mid-Atlantic States; their main charge was to watch and counter and/or fight the main British Army under Howe's command. On average, Washington was lucky to have about 10,000 men.

Another Army, now mostly state militia, served the Carolinas and Georgia. That Army was not active right now because the British were elsewhere. In 1776, this army was able to repulse a British invasion at Charleston, South Carolina, with help from General Charles Lee. Other famous generals from the south included Francis Marion, Andrew Pickens, William Moultrie, Thomas Sumter, Richard Henry Lee, and Lighthorse Harry Lee – the father of Robert E. Lee.

The third Army, the Northern Department of the Army, was much like the second one. It was established early in the war to protect the water route to Canada from Fort Ticonderoga to Lake Champlain to Lake George to the St. John River. It consisted of local troops as well as the remnants of several armies sent against Canada on previous campaigns. It's commander from the start was Major General Phillip Schuyler, a descendant of the Old Dutch patroons of the Albany area.

This Army, however, was terribly divided by regional loyalties and interregional disputes. One major cause of these disputes was the Green Mountain region known as the Hampshire Grants, the land that became known as Vermont. The land claimants from New York looked to Schuyler for leadership on the grants matter.

The New Englanders for some reason found a leader in Granny Gates. Granny took this role seriously enough to leave the field and plead the case before Congress. It was work he knew well.

Gentleman Johnny Invades

Everything was going well for 'Gentleman Johnny' Burgoyne at the beginning of his march south. He sliced through American defenses everywhere he found them. He enjoyed gourmet picnics during day marches and his tent at night was like a lively London literary son.

He took Fort Ticonderoga without firing a single shot when his men put a gun battery on the summit of Mt. Defiance across the narrow lake. The Americans thought the top was inaccessible. They were wrong. It commanded the fort and the Americans fled.

After the Ticonderoga victory, however, the wheels began to come off his wagons.

Oriskany

A secondary expedition under Colonel Barry St. Leger had been sent down the Mohawk River Valley from Oswego toward Albany to disrupt and destroy farms and settlements in that rich agricultural region. Composed mostly of American Indians, this column inflamed the valley when the Mohawks were unleashed and civilians were massacred. Local residents raised a New York militia army under command of General Nicholas Herkimer. On August 6, 1777, these Dutch farmers defeated St. Leger at the Battle of Oriskany, and sent the British back to Canada. General Herkimer died of his wounds after the victory.

Bennington

Another expedition was sent to the Hampshire Grants to find feed and horses for a dismounted brigade of Hessian dragoons.

Washington's Savior

Hessians under Colonel Friedrich Baum, who spoke no English, led the incursion force. New Hampshire militia Colonel John Stark, a veteran of Boston and Bunker Hill, and Colonel Seth Warner, formerly of the Green Mountain Boys, quickly recruited a large force of volunteers for local defense. They pursued the Germans and then shattered them at the Battle of Bennington, in Vermont, just ten days after Oriskany on August 16th.

These defeats bothered Burgoyne, but he also had other problems as well. He was still waiting to hear what Howe was going to do when he decided to march his 8,000 men, some 20 remaining miles to the Hudson and then move on Albany, over an old abandoned road rather than portage the army a few miles to the Hudson.

They had to use a road that in 1757 was the site of the massacre at Fort William Henry, and time had not yet removed all the reminders of that horror.

Rotting wagons littered the over-grown roadway, as did the bones of the victims and their pack animals. In addition, veteran woodsmen from Schuyler's army kept felling trees all along the road to make it hard for the British to keep moving.

Finally, on July 30th, 1777, an exhausted John Burgoyne limped into an abandoned, ramshackle edifice called Fort Edward, not far from Lake George. Like Ticonderoga, Edward was a leftover from the old French wars that finally ended in 1760 with the French surrender of Montreal and their complete

173

loss of North America. But unlike stone Ticonderoga, Edward's fortifications were parallel log walls between eight and 12 feet apart, then filled in with earth. Much of the old fort was rotting and way beyond repair. Burgoyne got his men inside to take advantage of the little protection provided by crumbling Edward and catch their breath for a few days. It would have to do.

The Americans Arrive

General John Glover received his orders to move to the north on July 23rd and by the 27th, he was watching several sailing ships, carrying his soldiers, move away from the Peekskill docks out into the current of the Hudson River. Glover knew that the river could get his men there much faster than by marching through the woods.

He himself followed the next day by boat.

At the American camp, he found that Washington also had sent John Nixon and his brigade north. They both were sympathetic to General Schuyler and his position with the army and they both wondered what was going on with General Gates.

On August 6th, Glover wrote a long and frightening letter to James Warren, a member of the Massachusetts General Court, representing Marblehead. In the letter, he listed a number of New England regiments whose enlistment expired at the end of the month. The need for replacements or reinforcements was growing urgent, and Glover was placing responsibility directly on the state government for help.

Glover continued:

> Reinforcement lays with you and not with us. If we
> fly before the enemy, it will be for lack of men. You
> may rely on that. We shall; not turn our back on
> equal numbers...General Schuyler tells me he has
> written to the Assembly of our state repeatedly, but
> has not received an answer[48].

John Glover, like many others, feared the next battle of the Revolution might well be the last.

Several days later, two generals from Washington's command rode into camp and met with Schuyler. They were not sent to take over – Washington did not control that job, Congress did – but to study and give advice to Schuyler.

One of the two generals was not well known. The portly Benjamin Lincoln was a Massachusetts farmer, personally and militarily. Washington later trusted allow Lincoln to receive the surrender of Cornwallis at Yorktown.

The other general was much better known and the men who had served under him either loved or hated him – it was Benedict Arnold. He had served here and had led some of the men in the futile assault on Quebec City at the end of 1775. Others had served as sailors in the makeshift navy he had built and used on Lake Champlain to force Sir Guy Carlton to turn back to Canada in the fall of 1776. There must be fighting ahead if they had sent Arnold.

Shortly after the generals arrived, a new

---

[48] Glover to James Warren.

contingent of soldiers marched into camp and they looked eerily familiar to General Glover and a few of his long-serving veterans. They were the white buckskin-clad riflemen from Virginia under the command of Colonel Daniel Morgan. These were the men of the 14th Massachusetts, who had brawled with, in that field near Harvard College more than two years ago during the siege of Boston. Although there had been conflicts in the past, Glover and his men were extremely glad to see the Morgan's men march into camp. Daniel Morgan was fighter and veteran of the war, as far back as, Arnold's assault on Quebec in 1775.

Benedict Arnold would again find value in Morgan's fighting spirit.

Chapter 17

Saratoga Prelude

As soon as Glover's Brigade had arrived at the camp of the Northern Army at Van Schiacks's Island in the Hudson, they were sent out to fight by General Schulyer.

They were assigned to their own section of the defensive line near the far right end of the defensive perimeter. The fighting arrived and overtook them quickly.

Almost hourly, they were engaged in skirmishes or attacks or counterattacks that gave them very little peace at any hour of day or night. Glover wrote to his brother Jonathan that his men were fighting a new enemy.

In Boston, New York, and New Jersey, he noted, they fought Englishman and Hessians; but here in the wilds of New York, they were locked in mortal combat with the original enemy – the American Indian.

"We were constantly in an alarm," he wrote on August 6, 1777. "Our scouting parties for the most part, cut off, killed, scalped and taken prisoner" he added. He also told the family that he and his men had arrived at Saratoga along with great droves of cattle, sheep, and swine. At least they would not go hungry.[49]

---

[49] Glover to family, 8/6/1777, Upham, p. 24.

Washington's Savior

It is no surprise that the Indians and their style of fighting bothered Glover. When the colonial militias were first started, they were designed to defend settlements from Indian raids. The members learned Indian tactics and how to defend against them so they could save their homes and family. But as the frontiers went further and further west and away from the oriments, so did the Indians. As they did, the militias became both more ceremonial in nature – and much less familiar with their reason for being – Indian fighting.

In fact, it had been more than a century since the Marbleheaders had last heard a bloodcurdling war whoop within a hundred miles of the town green, but it was only months ago that they had faced down the Redcoats in the Salem Alarm. They were no longer trained to oppose the Mohawks. They were now transplanted Europeans trained by Europeans to defeat Europeans in North America.

Indians Choose Sides

The Indians were having problems of their own. When the French left America in 1760 after New France was absorbed by British North America and Native tribes lost their only friends and defenders. Now they had to choose between the hated British and the damned settlers who stole their land, the Americans, who they called the Long Knives. Again, they looked at the British strength – their forts, their endless armies, their cannons and guns, and their overall superiority.

After several months of wrangling, most of the Indians chose between the Redcoats and the Long Knives.

They chose wrong again.

The Indians fought in several early battles with the English, but after a number of defeats and some heavy casualties, more and more Indians slipped away night after night and went back to their villages. There they kept the frontiers on fire for years to come.

By 1779, Washington had had enough. He himself led a strong segment of his Army through the Indian villages along the Wyoming River in Pennsylvania. They burned crops, destroyed villages, and began the process of removing the Native inhabitants from their lands with food, shelter and land foolishly promised. Their dreams would become living nightmares. Washington himself was called "the destroyer of villages."

Glover Writes Home

It was during the later weeks in midsummer of 1777 that Glover began to assault his brother Jonathan and his old friends Elbridge Gerry and Azor Orne with a litany of letters complaining about a wide variety of problems over which he or they had little or no control.

Things like the quality of his troops, the quality of their leadership, the quality and quantity of their supplies and equipment, and the quality and superiority of their foes. He seemed, by a reading of his words, to be confused and concerned. He was not the same John Glover of the East River or of the Delaware.

Fears Boston in Grave Danger

This was also during the time when Howe and his fleet were still somewhere in the Atlantic and that fact alone developed in Glover a major concern for the fate of Boston. Until Howe reappeared, heading for Philadelphia, Glover remained convinced a return attack on Boston was inevitable.

On July 25, he informed his brother about a report on a 'Mr. Williams' who was supposedly gathering all the small boats and local pilots he could find along Long Island Sound so General Howe's transport fleet could rendezvous with them when they tuned north to ravish the capital of New England.

Glover's fierce pen continued:

> It's one of the first principles of war to deceive. Howe has taken great pains to do this in many circumstances; his expedition he still keeps a profound secret, at the same time offers great encouragement for pilots to the southward, gives prisoners opportunity to escape, with the design that this be known to General Washington...All of these maneuvers are designed to deceive us. I wish the effect would not prove it. If his objective were Philadelphia, would he have not procured pilots in a more appropriate manner?

The more he wrote, the more adamant he became, telling his readers in Marblehead they should take his letter as a dire warning and should sound the alarm throughout the state before it was too late.

"I would not be understood to dictate," he wrote, "But sir I think it advisable that the state militia should be placed on a respectable footing, ...By all means, meet them if possible at their the British landing." [50]

Glover was not shy about arguing on this subject with the Army staff as well. He truly felt Boston would be Howe's next target and a target of revenge.

Before he left Peekskill, he wrote to Timothy Pickering, Washington's adjutant general, about his reassignment to the north.

Glover wrote that "should the enemy be gone to N. England, which from many circumstances I believe they are, I shall be very unhappy; beg you should use your power to have us recalled and join the part of the Army assigned to oppose them."[51]

It apparently did not elicit a response because everyone else but Glover recognized that Howe definitely was going for a war-ending swoop on the rebel capital.

It may be Glover feared for the safety of his family or what little business he had left behind, and there is no doubt he truly cared about his friends, neighbors, and his state, but he swore a typical blue streak in this case that General Howe was coming back to Boston to have his revenge for the humiliation of Bunker Hill. Maybe he just wanted to go home.

---

[50] John Glover to Jonathan Glover, 7/25/1777, Upham, p. 25.
[51] Glover to Timothy Pickering, 7/23/1777, p. 26.

Howe himself ended the debate when, in early August, the word reached the American high command that Howe and his fleet had reappeared off the Delaware Capes. That answered the question of where – it could only be Philadelphia.

Schuyler and Glover

Strange as it may seem, Schuyler may have had a hand in some of these letters that John Glover wrote and sent to his brother and other key people in Marblehead. Unfortunately, General Philip Schuyler was roundly hated in New England over the Hampshire Grants questions and his constant support of the New York position. And both men realized the army needed re-supply from the east.

Schuyler was dependent on supplies and reinforcements from two largest states in his territories – New York and Massachusetts. In point of fact, the latter sent him little and the General held no power over them.

Because Washington and Schuyler had worked together since 1775, they had actually become friends. While there is no proof of such a conversation-taking place, it would not have been a surprise if the tall Virginian had told the older, bald New Yorker that he could trust the short, taciturn and sometimes outspoken brigadier from Marblehead, Massachusetts. So it would seem logical that he would seek some assistance from General Glover.

On August 6th, Glover wrote another

strongly worded, yet polite letter to his brother Jonathan and this time to Elbridge Gerry. Again, he outlined the difficulties and challenges he felt the Continental Army was facing, as well as the traditional cost of fighting a forest war. Glover noted at the end of the letter that "General Schuyler tells me he has written repeatedly to our General Court but has received no answer."

Glover no doubt wanted to get those rich merchants in New England – the ones he had defended in Boston and Beverly – to open up their cargo holds and provide the supplies and munitions they had promised – or at least let Schuyler know why they wouldn't.

In one of the other letters, this one dated September 5th, 1777, Glover had written some unusual personal commentary. He wrote about a phaeton, a type of elegant horse-drawn carriage that he owned and was willing to let his friends back home use – but with a caveat.

"At present," he wrote, "I am not inclined to sell it, but should he (his brother Jonathan) not see me again, my desire is that he may have it, paying the value to my wife for her and the children's support."

Then Glover added what for him was an unusual personal addendum.

> My compliments to your good ladies and families and my old friends the Tuesdays Club, including the Rev. Messrs. Whitwell and Story, one of whom I expected and would have been happy to have had as a chaplain to my brigade, for want of which I have to do my own preaching.
>
> They possibly can do more good at home and I am

sure they will not have more exposure and will live better.[52]

You can almost hear in your reading of this letter the feelings of homesickness, loneliness, jealousy and despair that undoubtedly afflicted Glover during that part of his career.

Gates Takes Charge

On August 19th, Horatio Gates rode into camp bearing instructions about a change in command of the entire army. Now he, not Schuyler, was in charge of turning back Burgoyne.

The change in command was cordial and even polite, considering the temperament of the officers and the men involved in the command structure. To coordinate the change in leadership, even though he was the odd man out, Schuyler offered to brief Gates and his staff on the situation they faced. The next day, Schuyler left camp and all of its problems to Gates.

It appears that Glover and Schuyler had a brief yet friendly relationship in the few days before war drums began again. On August 22, three days after the dismissal, Glover wrote to Albany to thank the general for small kindnesses, including some tobacco, wine and fresh-churned butter that Schuyler had sent Glover and his men when they first arrived.

---

[52] Glover to Jonathan Glover, 9/5/1777, Upham, p. 28.

But the Marblehead general provided him with additional information out of loyalty and friendship. If Granny had known, he probably would have court-martialed Glover.

He wrote:

> General Gates has made preparations to advance, but not until he is properly reinforced. Scouting parties kept out all the time; some returned last night; no account of the enemy's approaching this side of Saratoga.
>
> Adieu my dear Genl., and believe me to be with esteem and team in respect your most humble and obedient servant.[53]

Schuyler had been able to give Gates the news about flinty New Hampshire General John Stark and his victory over the Hessians at Bennington in the Hampshire grants. That news worked up the flagging spirits of soldiers throughout the camp.

Gates Makes a Difference

Then, something strange happened after Schuyler left. Suddenly the army became happier, showed much less antipathy toward command and began to take shape as a much more efficient and disciplined body, one that Glover now thought might even be able to deal with the fast-approaching Burgoyne and his army.

---

[53] Glover to Schuyler, 8/22/1777, Upham, p. 27.

Glover at first was loath to admit it, but the difference was Horatio Gates. It turned out that when he wasn't stabbing people in the back and when he was doing something he enjoyed, Granny could be very pleasant.

As one historian wrote – "Gates, whatever his shortcomings, was jolly and kindly."[54]

Gates had done well with the Continental Congress. He had convinced them Schuyler was responsible for the loss of Fort Ticonderoga, even though he had been miles away when the stupidity of men like General Arthur St. Clair took center stage when they decided no guns could ever reach the wooded summit of Mount Defiance.

He must have been very persuasive with the lawmakers, because when he arrived to take over the Northern Army, he now had an independent command, reporting to Congress and not George Washington. Apparently Gates had widespread support among New England delegates, including even John Adams, who seemed to favor actually replacing Washington.

Two other moves helped to cement Gates' immediate popularity.

First, he re-organized the army into a three grand-division structure, taking advantage of the talents of the various officers he now had on his staff. For command of the right, Gates chose Major General Benjamin Lincoln, a portly former farmer from Massachusetts.

Gates himself in would take the center, which included Glover's brigade, Nixon's brigade,

---

[54] Ward, vol. 2, p. 500

and several other Continental line outfits, many of whom had bristled under Schuyler but were happy to serve Gates. In spite of his career in the British army, Gates had very little combat experience and he had never commanded a unit this big in combat.

In 18th century armies, command of the left wing of an army usually went to the most senior officer or the best fighting general. In this case, command of the left went to Major General Benedict Arnold. Also, under Arnold, were the crack fighting units led by Daniel Morgan and Henry Dearborn. They had fought together in the snows of Quebec in 1775.

The second thing Gates did for the army was to give it a permanent defensive home. Under Schuyler, the army had been going up and down the river trying to anticipate Burgoyne and his every movement along the Hudson.

Gates, however, was a defensive-minded general, and with the help of volunteer Polish engineer Thaddeus Kosciusko, he developed an intricate series of deeply dug trenches and gun emplacements on Bemis Heights in Saratoga, a place they would all know very well within the next few weeks.

Glover's Challenge

On September 10th, John Glover was given a command challenge. Ever since he had rejoined the army in June, Glover's Brigade had consisted of four under-strength Massachusetts regiments – Voses's First, Shepherd's Fourth, Wigglesworth's

Thirteenth, and Bigelow's Fifteenth. All good, tough, patriotic, professional men of the line.

Now to fill in Glover's extremely thin ranks, Gates assigned three New York militia regiments from Albany, Whiting, and Dutchess counties to the brigade. All good men, tough, patriotic, citizen soldiers. But the merging of these troops was an immediate recipe for disaster.

First of all, the New Yorkers hated the New Englanders as if it were their birthright, while the New Englanders abhorred their hosts with rival vitriol. Second, the disciplined Continentals had little respect for the militia and their frequent lack of social and military manners. The militia in all armies of the world disliked regulars – in this case, the militia said the regulars were no better than the Red Coats.

Finally the Yorkers saw the command structure of what they had perceived to be their own northland army and cringed at the names of those who now topped it commanded it – Gates, Arnold, Lincoln and Glover – all from that damn New England.

Fist fights and brawls, as well as other more serious struggles, took place hundreds of times; so often that Glover threatened to take any offenders – no matter if they were colonels and majors or corporals and privates, dump them into solitary confinement gaol's and pillories and throw away the keys.

Thankfully, this situation did not last long – Johnny Burgoyne had broken free of the wilderness and was moving south.

Washington's Savior
Burgoyne Stretches for Albany

John Burgoyne moved forward in his attempt to take Albany. He had solved many of the problems that plagued his army at Fort Edward, and it did not take long for them to reach the Hudson, about 50 miles from his objective. Once he reached that river, he realized that he was on the wrong side to attack the city. He would have to cross the river sooner or later – he chose sooner.

Burgoyne also knew that crossing the river would put him on the same side as the American army and it would make a battle inevitable. He knew they were entrenched somewhere ahead, but he had something else up his sleeve.

Burgoyne and Gates were no strangers – in the small world of the 18th century British army's officer corps that often times was impossible. In fact, they were close comrades for several years during the Seven Years War, 1754 to 1761. He knew that Gates would rather stay behind walls rather than come out fight in the open.

In spite of Burgoyne's public bluster and his absolute refusal to retreat, Gentleman Johnny was worried. He was in the New York woods in September with no winter quarters to go to. He could not return to Canada and command self-respect. Right now, his best – his only hope – was Albany.

On September 13th, Burgoyne had engineers build a bridge of boat across the Hudson River – much like Xerxes the Persian emperor, bridged the Hellespont as he made his road to Europe in his unsuccessful bid to conquer the free Greek city-states in 480 B.C.

It took them several days to move the approximately 8,000 men under Burgoyne, their equipment and baggage across the Hudson, but soon it would be done and he would be able to re-form his army. Unlike Xerxes, Burgoyne had his engineers take the bridge apart and turn it back into boats. It was a signal to his men that he would not be returning this way no matter takes place ahead.

They marched south.

Chapter 18

'Rabble in Arms'

When he first saw his rebellious foe drawn up in battle lines, Johnny Burgoyne told his staff they were facing nothing but a 'rabble in arms.'

The name seemed to fit the Northern Army and it was remembered and perpetuated over the years. In 1933, author Kenneth Roberts immortalized the words by using them as the title of his outstanding novel of Saratoga – *Rabble In Arms.*

It was a fitting sobriquet for both.

The battle of Saratoga took nearly a month to complete. Real fighting started on September 19; Burgoyne surrendered on October 17th. In the interim the two armies fought at Freeman's Farm and at Bemis Heights. These two battles, added to the conflicts at Oriskany and Bennington and the British thrust at Ticonderoga, made up the entire Saratoga campaign.

The First Day of Battle – Freeman's Farm

By September 18th, Burgoyne was about two miles away from the American lines on Bemis Heights at Stillwater, about four miles to the north of Saratoga.

On September 21st, John Glover again took up his pen to tell his family and friends back in Marblehead, especially his brother Jonathan and his friend and community leader Azore Orne, about this first phase of the battle and how the Northern Army was performing.

The first day was September 18th. Glover wrote "we marched out with 3000 men to engage the enemy who were encamped on a height about 2 miles from us; it was not practical because they had taken a more advantageous post;....We tarried there until dark and did nothing more."[55]

The next day was different. The British were rested and their ration fires had burned late into the night as the soldiers cooked their food for the next portion of their final march.

On September 19th, Burgoyne was determined to break through the works at Bemis Heights, determined to smash through those blue lines before the day was done and then he could move on Albany. It also appeared that Burgoyne knew Granny better than he had expected – the old girl had no intention of fighting a battle that was offensive in nature.

The fight focused on the left side of the American line. It seemed that three British columns led by Burgoyne, General Simon Fraser and Hessian Baron von Reisdel were totally determined to break through the part of the line being held by Benedict Arnold.

Glover's brigade and many of the other

---

[55]Glover to Jonathan Glover, et al. 9/22/1777 Upham, p. 29.

Washington's Savior

Continental units were assigned defensive positions on the right side where General Lincoln should have been. But Lincoln was in Vermont, recruiting farm boys to be soldiers. Gates had taken over Lincoln's command and he would not go on the offensive at all.   Arnold, meanwhile, was responding in kind. That volatile leader fought Burgoyne's aggressive movements, blunting each and every one during the long morning of fighting. Arnold's loyal regiments from New Hampshire and New York would do anything for him because he would do anything them. He thundered across the battlefield on his horse like an Old Testament prophet fighting the Philistines. But the enemy fought back, and they fought back hard.

Arnold kept asking for Gates to release the reserve to him so he could put Burgoyne away once and for all. He begged, telling Gates that victory was so close he could taste it.

Gates refused.

Then, late in day, Gates released Morgan and his riflemen, but it was too late. After some of the heaviest rifle fighting of the war, Arnold and the Americans were forced to disengage and move back to the protection of Bemis heights.

Glover wrote:

The battle was very hot till half past 2 o'clock, ceased for about half an hour, then renewed his attack. Both armies seemed determined to conquer or die. One continual blaze, without any intermission till dark when, by consent of both parties, it ceased. During which time we several times drove them, took their ground, passing over great numbers of their dead and wounded. Took one field piece, but the woods and brush were so thick, and being pushed by another enemy unit coming up, was obliged to give up our prize. The enemy in their turn sometimes drove us. They were bold, intrepid, and fought like horses, and I do assure you sir, our men were equally bold and courageous....We took about 70 prisoner, among which are two officers.[56]

In the same letter, Glover provided some clue of the cost of the day, noting that Gates' army that day suffered 202 wounded and 191 killed or missing. Among those dead were Lt. Colonels Cobwin, Adams and Lt. Thomas, while Captain Allen and Ensign Foster were also killed. Captain Bell was mortally wounded.

Both armies expected the other to attack. But neither did. Their camps made lots of noise, but both armies stayed put.

Between the Engagements

Changes now took place within the armies that were stalemated along the Hudson River as late September turned into October and thoughts turned to winter snow.

First, Glover and Gates quickly developed their relationship into a friendship that lasted though the war years and to their deathbeds. Gates may well have had less than pure motives for doing this, but Glover never was implicated in any kind of anti-Washington activities. To him, the friendship was real. Glover died in 1797; Washington in 1799; and Gates in 1806.

---

[56]Glover to Hannah Glover et al, 9/221/1777, Upham, p.30.

Washington's Savior

Second, General Benjamin Lincoln arrived back in camp from his recruiting trip in Vermont and brought with them a large number of new soldiers. Gates now had more than 11,000 troops to face Burgoyne's dwindling force, now about 7,000. It could be an overwhelming number.

Third, the relationship between Gates and Arnold went from a small brush fire to a raging conflagration. The Connecticut general was already angry with Gates for not supporting him with more men during the Freeman's Farm fight. Gates, in turn, threatened to replace him withoy Lincoln or someone else. Then Gates began to bait Arnold by telling him he was reassigning his best troops – Dan Morgan's and Henry Dearborn's – to someone else. Gates even transferred four New York regiments to Glover's control; when Arnold confronted Gates, Granny said it was a clerical error and said it was a mistake, a 'miss-assignment.'

But the rage reached hurricane levels when Gates wrote an action report about the battle and sent it to Congress. In that report, Gates did not once mention the names of Arnold or Morgan or Dearborn, no matter how much they did to turn the tide of battle. When Arnold found out, the arguments began all over again. Using the crudest language they could muster, the two men argued for hours until finally Gates fired Arnold and confined him to his tent.

Frustrated, slighted and nearly insane with his blinding rage, Arnold was packing when a group of his officers brought him a petition asking him to stay. Every officer in the camp but Gates and Lincoln signed it. Arnold stayed.

On the other side of the fighting line, Burgoyne was swallowing hard too. Local Tories brought him news that Sir Henry Clinton had left New York and was moving up the Hudson with a small force.   But then he got more news that local patriot militia in Westchester County met Clinton.   They blocked his way, so Clinton, who could not afford to lose New York, turned around to protect it. Burgoyne would receive neither help nor reinforcements.

In the weeks between battles, John Glover tried to keep his family up to date with the fighting in the north woods of New York.   On September 29th, he again wrote to his family and friends and apologized about his lack of writing. He continued:

> The enemy has remained very quiet, about one mile distant...we have taken 30 prisoners since the battle, and as many more deserted. Our men are in fine sprits, are very bold and daring, a proof of which I will give you in an instance two nights past.[57]

It seems General Glover suggested to Gates that the Americans make frequent scouting probes that would test Burgoyne's perimeter, and would keep the British up all night while being reminded the whole time of what a predicament they were in.   Granny thought it was a fine idea and told Glover that he should lead the first one on Sept. 27.

---

[57] Glover to Jonathan Glover and family, Upham, p. 30-31.

> I ordered 100 men from my Brigade to take a picket of about 60 of the enemy, who were about a half mile from me, at the same time ordering a cover party of 200 to support them by myself. The night being very foggy an dark, could not find the enemy until the break of day. When we made the proper disposition for the attack, they went on like so many tigers, bidding defiance to musket balls and bayonets. Drove the enemy, killed 3, wounded a great number.[58]

Glover and his men captured packs and kits off soldiers and found them empty of food. Burgoyne was starving.

This caused the Americans to tighten the noose on the British. They continued the daily raids on the perimeter started by John Glover, and Burgoyne later admitted that lack of sleep highlighted by these raids quickly became problem for all.

Meanwhile, the American army was growing as more and more militia units came to help, much as they did at Boston. Burgoyne knew time was running out. On October 4, the British held a war council and it was decided they would attempt their breakout on October 7.

A Brighter Outlook

Throughout this later period of the Saratoga campaign, Glover was much more optimistic about the pending outcome of the fighting at Bemis Heights, much more than during his time at Peekskill and the Jersey camps. "God grant that every man do his duty, and be crowned with

---

[58] Ibid.

success...I am fully satisfied that they will fight hard when their time comes" he wrote that same day.

Bemis Heights

This fight – the second half of the Battle of Saratoga – sealed Burgoyne's fate.

He found he could not break out while the Americans could break into his lines. He lost many good men who could not be replaced – men like General Simon Fraser who was felled by American sharpshooters.

This was not supposed to be a very difficult campaign. His elite regiments should have should sliced right through the damn rebel lines like they did before Ticonderoga. And Burgoyne had a pretty good idea which rebel general was bogging down his chance to escape this day – it must be Benedict Arnold.

Almost Picture Perfect

A newspaper artist trying to illustrate the battle of Bemis Heights for American readers had two contrasting images to consider. The first is more of a still photo, an oil painting of General Horatio Gates. Smugly sitting in his headquarters with his staff, waiting to review battle reports rather than going out in to the battle to see to see for himself.

The second is more of an action video of a single man on a brown horse, thundering across the battlefield, urging men to unite and 'follow me,' and leading them to assault Burgoyne's works until finally a bullet strikes him, he falls from the horse and the fighting ends for the day.

Two illustrations, but only one counted at the time. The unfortunate truth is that "to the victors goes the spoils," not to mention the ability to write the history of an event. That surely was the case at Saratoga. While thousands died to give true meaning to the revolution, while Benedict Arnold lay burning with fever, while hundreds were being buried beneath the thick rustic soil of New York, Horatio Gates was gathering all the heroic garlands he could get. Eventually Congress made Gates chairman of the board of war, which reported to Congress and which at least made him superior to Washington on the organization chart.

And where was John Glover during the struggle at Bemis Heights? He was there, but now, after more than 200 years of study and analysis, there is some question about what he and his brigade did. Whatever they did, surely it was done under orders that likely came directly from his boss, General Gates.

Some contemporary reports indicated that perhaps the only other general officer who performed better than Glover that day was Arnold himself. Nathan Sanborn in 1903 wrote that Glover had three horses shot out from under him during some of the heaviest fighting of the war. But other people wondered.

His predecessor as local Marblehead historian, William Upham noted that on October 7th, Glover's Brigade was a part of the reserves commanded by Benjamin Lincoln.

Glover himself wrote very little that still exists about his deeds at Bemis Heights that October day. Glover himself made no claim of personal heroism, but instead credits all battle success to "us," "we" or "the army". Not shy, Glover, in letters home, easily and eagerly grabbed credit for the raiding idea that Gates favored. But he is silent on Bemis Heights and that reinforces the idea that he was assigned to man the works with Lincoln and that is where he stayed.

Glover was no headline-seeking egomaniac, but he certainly would claim credit for things he had done that turned out well. But if he did not claim it, he probably did not do it.

John Glover, however, was not yet done at Saratoga.

Glover and the Ambush

Burgoyne and his army still had power and he knew his 5,000 men would fight for their lives. He still was able to retreat toward the north, without fear of hot pursuit from Gates, and, in particular, Arnold. By October 10th, Gates thought Burgoyne was all the way back at Fort Edward, and while some advance units were, the bulk of army lay just ahead.

In truth, however, most of Burgoyne's army was still in place and waiting for Granny's slow pursuit. Gates was slowly advancing on what he thought was a safe, broad front with Daniel Morgan on the left, then Learned's New

Hampshire brigade, John Nixon's brigade and finally Glover on the right. They all were attempting to cross the Fishkill, a stream that fed the Hudson.

As the units began to ford the stream, out of the corner of his eye, Glover saw what appeared to be a British soldier crossing the river in the wrong direction, toward the Americans. He ordered his men to capture him and bring him over for some direct questioning.

The soldier admitted that he was deserting, but he also had a dire warning for the Americans. He said Burgoyne had not retreated to Fort Edward, but was laying in ambush, waiting for an unsuspecting Gates to walk into his clutches.

Glover told the deserter he would be treated well if he had told the truth; otherwise he would hang. Then he went to work.

It was crucial now that Glover warn the other brigades about the ambush before it was too late. He sent a messenger to tell Nixon to cross back quickly before Burgoyne strikes and to spread the word to the other commanders. The message arrived in the nick of time; Nixon got his men back to the safe shore before the two sides could engage. In fact, if they had advanced another half-mile, they would have been caught in a horrible cross fire from 27 of Burgoyne's cannon, lined up and ready to fire. The ambush was foiled.

After this attempt, Burgoyne knew the game was over and it was time to go to Gates for terms. Once again, John Glover had saved the army.

Chapter 19

On the back roads of Massachusetts

Saratoga was one of the few key battles of the war that did not include at least one of the major belligerent armies stationed in North America.

Howe's army, of course, had gone to Philadelphia, while Washington and his Continental Army followed close on his heels. Howe defeated the rebels at Germantown and Brandywine Creek, the major encounters that were part of Washington's futile campaign to save the capital.

With fall disappearing quickly, both armies went into winter quarters to begin their military hibernation for the year. General Howe took advantage of the comforts provided by "the city of Brotherly love," while Washington went about 20 miles to the west to claim a place for his cold weather encampment. There, he could watch Howe and drill his men at a place called Valley Forge.

As the month of October wound down, Washington began to see and read fragments of action and casualty reports written and signed by Horatio Gates and speaking of a major victory at

Saratoga.

Washington knew that Gates was not sending information to him about the victory as part of the Gatesian campaign to take over the top job, Washington was furious and he was determined to do something about it. He already knew the basics about the battle – that Burgoyne was on the run and Arnold was severely wounded after winning on the battlefield; but it was the fact that Gates had insulted him that spurred him on.

Washington now sent his highest – ranking aide to get to the bottom of this. Colonel Alexander Hamilton, the future secretary of the Treasury and the man on the ten-dollar bill, brought a very personal verbal set of instructions for Gates that never again saw the light of day.

But his letter did.

Dated October 30th, 1777, the letter congratulates Gates flowingly and noting that this victory does the 'highest honor to American arms.'

> At the same time, I cannot but regret that a matter of such magnitude and so interesting to our General Operations, should have reached me by report only, or through the channel of letters not bearing the authenticity, which the importance of it required, and which it would have received by a line under your signature, stating the simple fact[59].

Washington had already been gracious and kind to Gates and his army weeks before when word and rumor of the great victory to the north reached his encampment.

"The General has the repeated pleasure of

[59] Washington to Gates, 10/30/1777, Lengel, p. 119.

informing the army of the success of the troops under General Gates over General Burgoyne," Washington wrote on October 15th, 1777.

"The General congratulates the troops on this signal victory," which Washington said was the third victory in the third quarter of the year. He went on to give fulsome praise all the officers and men for their bravery and determination.[60]

Burgoyne Gives Up His Sword

Back at the Saratoga camps, surrender day was scheduled for October 17th.

The formal ceremony took place on the battlefield, and the principals were a study in contrast – the victor Gates was ebullient, busy and solicitous; the loser Burgoyne was dour, cranky, and impatient to get this embarrassment over.

When Burgoyne surrendered his sword – which Gates quickly returned – a shout arose from the victorious forces that could be heard in Philadelphia by the Continental Congress and in Paris by envoy extraordinary Benjamin Franklin.

Franklin, the ultimate opportunist, was able to use the surrender to negotiate a treaty that would gain for the fledgling United States

---

[60] Granny would remain a thorn in the side of Washington until the Battle of Camden, South Carolina. Given the command of the Southern Army by Congress, Gates encountered Lord Cornwallis who thoroughly trashed the Americans in the beastly heat of August 15th. Gates fled at the first sign of defeat. He was said to have had the fastest horse in the army; he gave it no rest for 150 miles as he led the retreat.

soldiers, muskets, cannon, shells, French leadership, and most vitally, the use the French navy. The victory of Saratoga was more than a turning point, it was the beginning of the end.

Time would tell.

Solace for the Losers

Horatio Gates was nothing if not a wise and caring host and he showed it to his British and Hessian guests along the Hudson. Those captives could make up a spectacular dinner party because among them were ten generals and 14 members of Parliament.

As a result, Granny held a number of banquets to honor both winners and losers. During these banquets, Gates and Glover became very good friends with two of the highest-ranking enemy officer – John Burgoyne and the leader of the Hessian contingent, the Baron de Residel.

It also seemed like both American generals forgot for whom they worked. We have seen how Gates had ignored Washington in reporting his victory; now Glover failed to tell the commanding general about the new assignment he had agreed to take from Gates.

The Convention Army

The surrender instrument signed by Gates and Burgoyne was called the *Convention of Saratoga* and it would allow the American victors to send the vanquished army back to England if they gave their parole, an agreement not to take up arms against the Americans for the duration of the conflict. It would save Congress a lot of money.

Gates quickly agreed to the convention and that very same day, he handed the entire project off to someone he could trust – his new friend, General John Glover. It appears that Glover was pleased with the assignment, mainly because he wanted his next destination to be Boston and not a frozen campground in Pennsylvania.

There is little doubt that kindly Granny knew this was a legitimate way to get Glover home for at least a couple of days.

Glover wasted little time in organizing the England in two divisions. The British division of 2,442 men would travel through Northampton on its way to Worcester, where it would rejoin with the Hessian division of 2,198 men that had traveled by via Springfield. Glover said he would be leaving in the next few days and would accompanying General Burgoyne.

He expected that the various groups would arrive in Worcester in about 10 days and he asked that sufficient force be in that town to escort the defeated army into Boston safely.

Glover told Powell he was also arranging for food and provisions to be provided along the routes, and he suggested that the secretary begin to look for accommodations for the captured soldiers.[61]

In his memorial of Glover, William Upham notes that the Marbleheaders performed this duty

---

[61] Glover to Powell, 10/22/1777, Upham, p. 31.

with 'great kindness and skill.'[62]   In some ways Glover was unique in that he was one of the few generals to serve in the two battles of the Revolution in which the Americans took a large number of prisoners – Trenton and Saratoga.

Other historians are not quite so sure about his motive for doing so.

Dr. George Athan Billias, a noted scholar of the Revolution, a former professor at the University of Maine, and currently professor emeritus at Clark University in Worcester, MA, and the author of the 1960 book *General John Glover and his Marblehead Mariners*, outlines a laundry list of things Glover did wrong, concluding even that he was guilty of 'dereliction of duty.'[63]

Like so many things, the truth probably lies somewhere in the middle. Most of Billias' accusations are fairly easy to refute, and the dereliction charge is, in my opinion, absurd.

For example, when the Americans had the convention army attempt to cross the Hudson, only half made it that day – the 18th – because the captors had collected to few boats and they started crossing too late in the day.

Billias blamed Glover for the misstep, saying he was too concerned about being with Baron Residel that day and then joining him at General Schuyler's for a lavish dinner rather than handling at the crossing.   But at that point in time, Glover was taking over the entire project and he did not have the time to handle every facet

---

[62] Upham, p. 31.
[63] Billias, p. 151.

of the march. This did not cause a major problem for the army anyway, because by the end of the next day, everyone had crossed and they were on their way to Boston.

Also, from the simple perspective of protocol, it probably was necessary that some one of Glover's rank accompany the Baron all the way to Albany and to the Schuyler's. Glover would have been a natural choice for this, and it gave him a chance to thank and bid farewell to the still-influential General Schuyler.

Billias also felt Glover got a bit too cozy with the enemy-in-chief, Gentleman Johnny Burgoyne. He objected to Glover waiting several days after the prisoners began their march to leave with Burgoyne even after General William Heath, commanding in Boston, had named a special officer to accompany the defeated general. This was New Hampshire militia General William Whipple, who was also a signer of the Declaration of Independence and who knew neither Burgoyne nor the baron. No wonder Glover stayed.

Glover and Burgoyne Get Along Well

In reality, it may have come down to a personal choice over the escorts. If Glover made Burgoyne more at ease, then that was the right move to keep the two together.

It seemed the pair did get along well. In fact, Billias says, Glover even planned to take Burgoyne on a tour of the major port facilities between Boston and Portsmouth, N.H., to show

Washington's Savior

off the business strength of those communities.[64]

There even seems to have been some vague, foolish plan between Gage, Glover and Burgoyne that would have had the Marbleheader accompany Burgoyne all the way home to England. A letter from Glover to Gates mentions this proposed excursion – one that Glover may have anticipated eagerly – but there were too many factors involved in the deepening war that would make such a junket unseemly and impossible.

There seems little doubt that Burgoyne fascinated Glover – he would not have been the first to fall under the Englishman's unique spell. Gentleman Johnny was indeed a fascinating man. Few in the distant colonies had ever seen anyone quite like him – probably a royal bastard, a major general, a leader of men and a lover of women; a world traveler; a Member of Parliament; a playwright; a gourmet. He was a character unlike any other in the colonies – except for Dr. Franklin of course.

Even though Burgoyne and Glover got along well, they couldn't work out issues that eventually imprisoned the convention army. When the soldiers arrived in Boston, things fell apart when Congress asked Burgoyne for a list of his officers who would be on parole for their records and the General refused to comply.

When his stalemate continued, Congress finally refuted the convention in November 1777. The Congress sent Burgoyne's men more than 700 miles away to the area of Charlottesville,

[64] Billias. p. 151.

Washington's Savior

Virginia, to poorly built prisoner facilities. They remained there until 1781 and the surrender of Cornwallis at Yorktown. Many of the former British and Hessian soldiers decided to remain behind and become productive citizens of a new country.

The Baron von Steuben

While all this was going on in the north, George Washington was beginning a tough drilling program for the Continental army, thanks to a new volunteer, a baron and general from the famed army of Prussia.

Friedrich, Baron von Steuben, made a tremendous impression on Congress with his stories about Frederick the Great and his Prussian army. They sent him to Washington at Valley Forge with their highest endorsement.

The commander-in-chief was a bit more skeptical about the Baron's credentials, and he was proven right when it was later discovered that Steuben was not only not a 'von,' indicating nobility, he was not even a general. The highest rank reached in Europe was, like Horatio Gates, that of major.

But by that time, the army was trained and disciplined and ready to fight the enemy hold-up in Philadelphia. Washington by then did not care and he made the Prussian inspector general – a major general.

But now he wanted the rest of his army back together. Nixon's men had been back with the army for several weeks, but he had no word

from Glover or from Gates about Glover and his
men.

On January 8, 1778, he wrote to Brigadier
General Glover from the Valley Forge's camp.

> Sir,
>
> The time we to lay in winter quarters ought to be
> spent in training the men, and endeavoring to bring
> them into the Field in a more regular manner than
> they have hitherto been, I must desire you will join
> your brigade as soon as possible in order to effect
> this.
>
> I have another reason, which is that many of the
> Brigadiers and Colonels in my Command who have
> long been absent from their families have been
> under the necessity of going home to take care of
> their private affairs, that there are scarce officers
> sufficient to do the Camp duties much less make a
> proper arrangements should the enemy should come
> out to attack us. [65]

Washington certainly seemed to want
Glover back with his brigade for the special drill
instructions by von Steuben and to take his
rightful place with Continental Army as they
made plans for the spring. Washington fully
expected Howe to give up Philadelphia for the
comfort, security and safety of New York. He
would wait at Valley Forge for Howe to come out.
Washington was indicating he needed Glover to
come back so other field grade officers in arms
could do what Glover was doing – take care of
long-neglected affairs and matters at home.

---

[65] Washington to Glover, 1/8/1777, Upham, p. 32.

In fact one of the officers he noticed among the missing was his friend and compatriot John Nixon. Said to have suffered a partial loss of sight and hearing due to a cannon ball passing too close to his head at Saratoga, Nixon never again returned to active duty.

Glover also quickly realized Washington had no idea what he was doing with the convention army and he to get him the update he needed. Almost immediately, he responded with a lengthy letter that he sent off to Valley Forge via messenger on January 24th.

"I apprehend your Excell'y has not been fully acquainted with the Business I was charged by Genial Gates," Glover wrote. And, he continued, the business is still being attended to and will continue until General Burgoyne finally settles the cost incurred transporting his army home.

"I was honoured with the command of conducting him (Burgoyne) & his Troops from Saratoga to Cambridge," he wrote Washington, explaining how he divided the Convention Army into smaller divisions to ease the strife of making the trip with more than 5,000 prisoners.

Then he told Washington that he had to settle all accounts for the army's transit with Burgoyne before the defeated general takes ship home to Great Britain.

Furthermore, he told Washington:

The inhabitants look to me and expect that I shall see them paid. To acquit myself from censure, I'm determined to lay them before the General Court and desire that a committee be appointed to

213

examine them & and make what deductions shall appear to be just, which will give satisfaction to all parties. I shall waste no time bringing this to a close as soon as possible.[66]

It appears from letters written between Glover in New England and Washington at Valley Forge that while he was making some progress with the accounts, he could be doing much better. For example in one letter, Glover tells Washington he had met with Burgoyne the week before when a problem with the exchange rate cropped up. The English general wanted four Continental dollars for each pound charged. The Americans firmly said 'no' and another impasse took place. He didn't meet with Burgoyne again for a week.

As time went on, Glover carefully sprinkled his letters to the general with references to his growing ill health. On April 10th, 1778, he noted once again "in my last I wrote You Excellency of my ill state of health which does still remain."

By early April, Burgoyne had left Boston for the settlement of Newport in the tiny state of Rhode Island. From there, he took ship for England – another promising general ruined by America He would return home in disgrace. In London he had to face the commanders of the Army and King George III. He never received another army command.

Eventually Glover got the account situation to the point where just two of the towns through

---

[66] Glover to Washington, 1/24/1777, Upham, p. 32.

which the convention army had passed had not reached agreements with Glover and the British paymaster representing Burgoyne. But he also noted that the court hearings at one point were postponed for two long weeks because a small pox epidemic was sweeping through Massachusetts.

He then told Washington he was hoping to leave for camp by June 1st, but he added he was doubtful he could, in his current state, withstand the rigors of a new campaign.

> When I entered the service in 1775, I had as good a constitution as any man my age. But it is now broken and shattered to pieces. However, I shall make the best of it until I see your Excellency, when I flatter myself, from you generosity and humanity, you will not hesitate to favor my dismission from the Army.[67]

John Glover thought he knew his man in regards to Washington – he was sure he would let him go. But this time Glover guessed wrong. Again, he had underestimated the Virginian. He would not concur with "The desire you express of quitting the army," wrote General Washington. "I have too high of an opinion of your character. My earnest wish is that you continue."[68]

He rejoined the Army on June 28th.

---

[67] Glover to Washington, 5/15/1778, Upham, p. 35
[68] Washington to Glover, ibid.

Another Reputation Shattered

It was May 25th, 1778 and the ship, a speedy frigate, had just slipped away from the Philadelphia docks and was now gathering speed in the main current of the Delaware River. A man in a scarlet uniform stood on the quarterdeck next to the ship's captain, both men staring straight ahead.

General Sir William Howe finally had asked to be relieved as commander-in-chief of His Majesty's Forces in North America. He would not look one final time on the damned land – all it had done was to ruin his reputation. Forever.

It is ironic that it was the general most associated with the loss of America was the man who did the best in his post-colonial revolt career. In 1805, Charles, the Earl Cornwallis, was given the incredibly prestigious post of Viceroy of India by none other than King George III.

Chapter 20

John Glover and the Fight for Rhode Island

Known by a variety of names since it was built during one of the old French Wars, it was now named Fort Arnold, after General Benedict Arnold, the unsung hero of Saratoga, who was severely wounded in his leg as he led the American charge against the British redoubt at Bemis Heights.

Today, Glover would take command of Fort Arnold, having been on detached duty in Boston. After Saratoga, General Horatio Gates assigned him the task of escorting Burgoyne's defeated army to Boston. He then spent substantial time clearing up expenses accounts for the transit effort. Because of this, Glover never did join his brigade at any time during the Valley Forge campaign.

A Draw at Monmouth Courthouse

Ironically, his old fighting unit, Glover's 2nd Massachusetts brigade was in combat this same day with rest of the Continental

Army at the Battle of Monmouth Courthouse in New Jersey. This fight took place but a few miles from the Royal Navy at Sandy Hook and safety. People later said the day of the battle was the hottest in a century. Both armies sweltered in their wool uniforms, but Washington and his men didn't care. They had spent the winter at Valley Forge preparing for this moment training and drilling as unified military units with the erstwhile Baron von Steuben until the Prussian was blue in the face. They were ready for the British this time.

The battle started out with the normal attack of the Advanced Wing of the Continental Army, once again led by General Charles Lee, who had recently been exchanged by the British and returned to his command. Lee, however, was unaware of the improved military posture of his men and at the first sign of faltering, he ordered his men to retreat as he had in the past.

When a soldier told Washington that Lee's men were retreating, the General had him arrested for spreading lies. But when the Virginian found Lee moments later, he realized the soldier had not lied at all. Lee indeed was falling back.

A furious George Washington confronted him, allowed him no chance to explain, removed Lee from command immediately and sent him to the rear in disgrace. Lee never held another command; he died in Virginia in 1781.

Washington and the rest of his army re-engaged the British and the two sides fought the whole day under the unrelenting sun. In the early evening, the British were able to disengage and slip away to New York and safety.

Glover's brigade was part of the Right Wing commanded by Major General William Alexander, also known as Lord Stirling. Commanding the brigade was Colonel Bigelow, one of Glover's regimental commanders.

Glover in Charge at West Point

Safely ensconced in Fort Arnold, John Glover took stock of his command and he thought about what next steps to take. Although he was not an engineer, Washington had asked him to make changes were needed to bolster the defenses.

He also issue his first order of the day on the 28th using 'Washington' as the password and, ironically considering what would happen to the general that day at Monmouth. 'Lee' was the Countersign. The order itself read:

> General Glover acquaints the garrison that it's of the utmost importance that the works be finished as soon as possible; he therefore requests of Officers and soldiers that they exert themselves for that purpose. The Fatigue parties to begin work every morning at 5 o'clock, leave off at 10, begin again at 3 o'clock and work until sundown.

The General, fresh from months at home that seemed to revitalize his Congregational work ethic, was determined that his soldiers would be kept busy and their work would done right. He was amazed at how lax some things were. For example, in his second order of the day, he required all strangers and other unknown individuals stay out of the fort unless they had official business there and had a pass signed by an officer of authority.

He also sought out Thaddeus Kosciusko who had worked with Gates to fortify the Bemis Heights earthworks before the big battles at Saratoga. With the talented Polish volunteer doing the engineering and Glover managing the manual labor, much good work got completed quickly.

In early July, Washington and most of the army arrived back in the Hudson River, or the Highland, region. The last time the two men met face-to-face was something probably both would like to forget – when the 14th Continental regiment went home after Trenton. No one recorded what they said to each other, but once again they provided a stark study in contrast. Washington was tall, well dressed. Well-spoken. Healthy. Glover was short, taciturn, rumpled, had a thick New England accent, and his visage was twinged with illness.

Washington must have been pleased with work going on at Fort Arnold because he quickly found a new job for him. Glover was told to take command of Fort Clinton – named for Gov. George Clinton of New York – another decrepit link in the Hudson River chain of Continental fortifications.

The Rhode Island Campaign

Glover did not long remain at Fort Clinton,

however. The Continental Army finally was making its way north from the Monmouth area. Glover was ordered to find his unit on the road and then to join the division of the Marquis de Lafayette, who was also marching north with additional troops. The French nobleman was then ordered to proceed to Rhode Island and take part in a joint campaign with the French navy, under the overall command of Glover's old compatriot, Major General John Sullivan of New Hampshire.

Ever since Ben Franklin's treaty with France was announced in May, George Washington had been chomping at the bit to attack New York with the help of the French Navy. His loses in New York tormented Washington and would continue to do so for the duration. The Virginian eagerly awaited his chance to wreak vengeance on the city for the defeats he had suffered there in 1776.

The French, however, wanted no part of the complicated tides and channels of New York harbor. In addition, French Admiral Comte d'Estaing was only bringing twelve ships-of-the-line and four frigates and that would not be enough to fight the British fleet guarding that harbor. Their next choice was Newport, Rhode Island.

It was a good choice. Located on an island in Narragansett Bay, Newport was not only the sole British-held port between New York and Boston, it was the only garrison left in New England. It would be a good place to capture. After several planning sessions, the assault was scheduled for August 10th, with both American and French forces making simultaneous, amphibious attacks at separate locations.

But in the meantime, Glover received yet another special assignment, this time from John Sullivan. He was told to go to Boston and recruit up to 300 men who were expert seaman familiar with small boat operations. He was authorized to pay them up to three dollars per day, plus expenses, for up to three weeks work. Sullivan told Glover to get the men to Newport with all dispatch.

Glover did his work quickly.

Sullivan's order to Glover was dated August 1st; the recruits joined Sullivan before dawn on August 10th, the day of the scheduled assault. And it was an impressive group of sailors and boatmen, including what was called the 'Boston Independent Company' of militia, an entire company from Salem, and a large number of nautical experts from Marblehead.

Glover's boatmen were not the only troops on the roads in New England on those hot August days in 1778. A number of militia organizations from throughout New England were making their way to add their numbers to Sullivan's command. One such group's roster in particular contained names familiar to many, names not mentioned in revolutionary annals for several years – militia General John Hancock and Lieutenant Colonel Paul Revere. Neither would serve with great distinction in their only military appearance during the Revolution. After the war, Hancock served several terms as governor of

Massachusetts; Paul Revere went back to silver-smithing.

Also arriving in Rhode Island was native son General Nathanael Greene, sent by Washington to help Sullivan – and probably to watch over him as well.

Lucky John Sullivan

In retrospect, John Sullivan probably was not a good choice to command the Rhode Island expedition. It could be that Washington just wanted the loyal, yet volatile Sullivan out of his hair for a while and he sent him to Rhode Island to obtain that relief.

Sullivan was not a popular general nor a particularly good one. John Adams wrote to his wife the wished the first bullet fired at the Battle of Long Island in 1776 had gone through him.

Nor was Sullivan a diplomat. In many ways, he used hate to motivate himself. As the revolution had approached in the early 1770s, he learned to hate the British, much as he hated the French during the French and Indian War that ended in 1760. Some of that anti-French feeling may have lingered; it did not take long for the alienation to begin.

The joint attack fell apart quickly. Both forces were to attack the island on August 10th, but on the ninth, Sullivan noticed that the British general, Sir Robert Pigot, had moved some of his men out of his advanced works. Sullivan naturally sent some of his troops over to the island to occupy them.

Sullivan also named John Glover to command the forward position on the left wing, which would be led by the Marquis de Lafayette.

An Irritated Admiral

Admiral le Comte d'Estaing was upset when he found out about the unauthorized landing. He felt that he was the senior partner in the new alliance, and now this upstart colonial was trying to take over. He moved very slowly on August 10th in landing the 4,000 French soldiers he had brought with him. Then at about midday, the admiral sent a message saying a British naval squadron had been sited beyond the mouth of the Narragansett. He had recalled his landing force and re-boarded them. At dawn, on the 10th, the French weighed anchor to fight the British squadron, saying that was his first priority was to engage and destroy enemy warships. He would return as soon as he could.

Sullivan halted his attack, feeling he had no choice but to wait for the French. Then he reconsidered and decided that, since he already had taken the forward works, he might as well continue the general advance with his substantial armed force before the contrariness of the New England militia reared its ugly head and they pick up their muskets and go home.

But no troops attacked on the 12th; instead, a tremendous ocean storm roared into Narragansett Bay and kept the Americans in their lines and their tents and huts for two long, wet days. By the time the storm blew itself out, all the officers and men were wet, tired and heartily sick of Rhode Island.

Finally on the 15th, the dawn broke bright and clear and the morning air carried the promise of heavy humidity later in the day. In the morning sunlight the army advanced towards Newport.

Pigot by then had abandoned everything outside of Newport in preparation for what he expected to be a long siege. Pigot only had about a thousand men in his garrison so he was continually shortening his lines to conserve his defenders.

After marching a good distance that day with Glover leading on the left, they stopped about a mile and a half from the British lines at Newport. The Americans began to dig their defensive lines, and occupied them as they were completed, and then waited for their French naval allies. Those ships, the American generals felt, would be the difference between victory and defeat at Newport.

Glover, meanwhile, was temporarily assigned to Sullivan's staff and placed in command of the boatmen he had recruited from Boston. There is little doubt that he would plan and command amphibious operations during the campaign. Colonel Bigelow took over the brigade.

The Fleet Comes Back

That fleet flying the white fleur-de-lis flag of Bourbon France finally appeared in Narragansett

Bay on the 20th with news Sullivan did not want to hear. Admiral d'Estaing reported that several of his ships had sustained damage during the encounter his fleet had with a portion of Dick Howe's battle squadron from New York. But even worse things had happened.

The two-day storm that delayed Sullivan's attack was even more furious on the open sea. The gale-force winds tore away spars and riggings, swept sailors overboard, dismasted a variety of vessels and made a general mess of the fleet.

The admiral now was taking his wooden ships to Boston for repair. By the time that work was done, it would time to return the fleet to France and the other needs Louis XVI's Ministry of the Marine had for it. There would be no joint operation this year. In hours, the French were gone.

The Americans were flabbergasted this time. They could not believe what they were hearing from these so-called allies. Anti-French feelings ran rampant because all American officers and men knew they needed those beautiful, moveable, three-mast, floating gun platforms. And they wanted the help of the 4000 French troops that came with the ships. These disciplined soldiers would add great value to Sullivan's command, which exceeded 1,000 men, the vast majority of whom were untrained and inexperienced militia.

The Americans Confer

Washington's Savior

At a council of war, Sullivan asked his commanders for recommendations. Glover was not about to remain silent on this issue. He said there were two options remaining. The first option would be to institute a traditional siege with advancing lines. They would, however, have to take the chances of being caught out in the open by British reinforcements that they assumed were on the way.

The second option called for a series landings behind the lines that once completed, would provide a force to roll up the right flank as if it were ripe fruit. This plan might have worked, but desertions grew so fast that by the time they gave it serious thought, Sullivan decided there were not enough men to take the risk. It was said that on one day alone 500 men slipped away.

They knew, however, that without the French fleet and the 4,000 soldiers, they really had only one option – withdrawal, and a rapid one because if a British fleet caught them on the land, then the jig was up.

While waiting for the French, Sullivan already had his men dig a defensive line at the north end of the island near where they first crossed earlier in the month. Sullivan had supplies and equipment sent to the new line and then eventually to the mainland. Then, as dark fell on the evening of August 28th, Sullivan and his men left their fortifications, divided into three columns with each on a different road, and then turned north toward the mainland.

On the dusty East Road that night was the Marquis de Lafayette and his mixed division of

Continentals and militia. They marched quickly and quietly because they knew what would happen if the British caught them.

At the head of this column rode a short, stocky, shock-haired brigadier general in a uniform that was too small and riding a horse that was too big. John Glover was watching the marching troops like a deacon hovering over a church congregation in danger from the Devil looking for new souls.

In the wee hours of the morning of August 29th, the tired and weary American army arrived at the new defensive lines and quietly occupied them. Then they got ready to greet the British in case they paid a visit.

Back in Newport, it took General Pigot until morning to realize the Americans were gone, but he continued his cautious advance in case Sullivan was trying to lure him out into the into the open. When he was sure all was well, Pigot sent several units in pursuit of Sullivan along two of the roads used by the New Hampshire general. The force he sent along East Road was under the command of Brigadier General Francis Smith - of Lexington and Concord infamy. Smith and his men roared down the East Road, hoping to catch the rebels by surprise or at least before they dig in. They did neither.

At about 10 a.m., they were approaching what is called Quaker Hill when they saw what looked like a ragged scar running across slope off the high ground. The British were slowing just as several lines of soldiers rose up in unison from the scar and they heard John Glover yell 'fire!' as a heavy volley of American musket balls ripped through Smith's red coated detachment. They quickly took cover.

Throughout the day, Smith and other British officers tried to break the American lines to no avail. By 4 p.m. they decide to disengage and withdraw and wait for reinforcements.

John Sullivan gave great credit to Glover and his men during the Marblehead man's last combat of the Revolution. He wrote to Congress – "The Enemy advanced on our left rear but they were repulsed by General Glover."

The British disengagement gave Sullivan the chance to continue the withdrawal unmolested. Christopher Ward wrote in his *The War of the Revolution:*

> The cannonading from both sides was heavy for an hour, that of the Americans so discouraged Piget's troops that they failed to come to grips with Sullivan's. Desultory musketry continued between the two sides until it faded out at dark. In the night, Sullivan resumed his retreat as quietly as possible. John Glover's amphibious Marblehead regiment again proved its special worth in carrying the army across Howland's ferry to Tiverton where it was landed safety with all guns and baggage[69].

Different Directions, Different Duties

After reaching the mainland, the army split apart and dispersed. The remaining militia was

---

[69] Ward, p. 59.

dismissed and they went home to protect their farms and villages throughout New England and beyond.

The Marquis de Lafayette and Major General Nathanael Greene took most of the line Continental Army units and began the long hot march back to Washington's encampment on the Hudson River to keep watch on the British in New York.

The rest of the army – including John Glover's brigade – marched with Sullivan to Providence, the Rhode Island capital. In fact, this part of the army eventually became the Providence garrison, responsible for the safety of the city and surrounding territory. Glover's brigade would stay there until the middle of 1779.

Garrison Duty

For most of the war, they had been active soldiers, so Glover and his brigade found the duty troublesome and troublemaking. This assignment introduced Glover to many different things found in the seamier side of army life – things like mutiny, words never spoken in circles that included many colonels and generals.

Military mutiny has existed for as long as men have gathered in war-like formations and required discipline. Glover and his men – mostly seafarers – knew about naval mutiny like that which left Henry Hudson adrift in Hudson's Bay, or like the one which made Captain William Bligh a household name, or like the huge refusal of sailors to perform their duties at the Nore naval base that would so shape the Royal Navy in the years ahead. Most mutinies were caused by simple things and such things had afflicted the Continental Army, which had not been paid for many months. Food, shelter, uniforms and basic sustenance had been issues since Cambridge.

Mutiny first raised its ugly head in early September when a great – yet unspecified by Glover – disturbance affected his men. Always a disciplinarian but never a martinet, he took action to fight any trend toward disobedience. He found more for his men to do. He increased roll calls, made his officers keep better watch on their men, and tried to obtain better food and living conditions.

The Ultimate Tragedy

As the year of 1778 drew to a close, perhaps the cruelest of all personal tragedies struck John Glover and his family.

He happened to be at home on leave when on November 13th, his beloved wife of 24 years, Hannah, unexpectedly passed away at age 45. Glover had honored her in 1775 when he selected his schooner – the *Hannah* – to be the first ship commissioned in Washington's navy.

Even before her husband left for war in 1776, Hannah had been somewhat sickly and her husband had been deeply concerned about her health. Her health had been one reason why he tried to stay home from the army in 1777.

Details of her passing are sketchy, but we know that her life had become much more difficult since her husband went to war. She not only had to care for the family home, but she had to practically raise all the Glover children herself, including their education and religious training. She also handled John's business and keep food on the table for the entire family. To say Glover was devastated by her passing was a tremendous understatement.

<u>Chapter 21</u>

Home, Not So Sweet...

Ever since the battle of Trenton, John Glover's enthusiasm for the war and the grand experiment known as the American Revolution had been fading.

He still valued the cause of freedom, because he wanted self-determination for himself and his family, and he wanted nothing more to do with the English.

He truly wanted the British gone and gone for good. He was, he admitted to himself, a true patriot; he was proud of his own war record and also proud of what Marblehead and Massachusetts contributed to the war. He was glad he had gone to war, but now the price was getting too high. For the rest of his military career, he will do his most vigorous work trying to end it.

Glover thought he had hurt when his son was declared lost at sea, but that pain was nothing compared to what he felt like at Hannah's death. Her quick and sudden passing had crushed the entire family. And it made Glover believe he could not go on.

Thank God above, he was home when all

this took place, he thought. He would have been disconsolate if he could not have attended her funeral. While home in Marblehead, Glover buried Hannah, made an attempt to get out of the army, and arranged for the proper care of his children. He had eight still at home, none older than 17.

Glover was back in Providence in late January when he finally sat down to write to Washington to tell his commander-in-chief what had happened to his family. He told Washington that his Continental Army service was the most important thing he had ever done. As a mariner, he had experienced the harshness of the British first-hand in his seagoing business, and he was proud to be a leader of the men from Marblehead as they stood up to King George. He also laid out on paper that he was more than willing to continue that meager service for his country as long as his countrymen wanted it:

> But it has been the will of Heaven I should feel the pang of separation, and part with a companion most dear to me and who, during my absence, the only support and stay of a family of eight small children, the oldest of whom is seventeen years; the care of which calls for my particular attention.
>
> Those being my present circumstances, which are distressing, I am, from a sense of paternal duty and regard that I owe my little flock, compelled, though with great reluctance and regret, to ask for a dismission from the service.[70]

Now the shrewd Yankee in Glover made an

---

[70] Glover to Washington, 1/28/1779, Upham, p. 35.

appearance. He knew Washington had no qualms about refusing such requests outright from officers who made them, so he asked that the general also share his request with the Continental Congress.

By turning down those resignations, Washington was not ignoring the personal problems of his officers, he was seeking simply to keep his best officers until the war was over. A part of Washington's genius with this was not to make them do anything he would not do himself. For example, during the eight years of war, Washington made just one trip to visit Mount Vernon, his home on the Potomac River. That was in 1781, when the army was close-by, laying siege to Yorktown.

Glover continued:

> I feel myself happy in being one of those who have stood forth in defense of the liberties of America; and be assured, Sir, that whenever her Hon' able representatives or your Excellency shall call for my exertions. I shall endeavor with cheerfulness to comply therewith.

Then he thanked him for all the kindnesses and favors Washington had show to Glover and to other family members including his brother, Jonathan, and his son of the same name, and for anything he had or would do to benefit the community of Marblehead.[71]

Once the letter was signed and on its way, there was little for Glover to do except wait for the General and Congress to decide if he could go

---

[71]Ibid.

home and go home for good.

Congress Rules on Glover Bid

For once it seemed like the Continental Congress had moved expeditiously when it ruled on John Glover's request to leave the army. It said no.

He was too valuable to retire.

When he heard about the decision, he no doubt saw the delicate hand of General Washington in the February 27th, 1779 ruling. Glover could not go, but it was a tempered hand because the Congress also took care of Glover.

The citation read as follows:

> **RESOLVED, that Congress, sensible of Brigadier General Glover's past merits, and in expectations of his future services, directs the Commander-in-chief to indulge him with a furlough for as much time as may be necessary to settle his private affairs.**[72]

All things seemed ready for Glover to pack up and take the 60-mile ride on horseback to Marblehead and finally have some lengthy time with his family. He just needed to tie some loose ends together at the encampment and he should able to leave quickly. But somehow things rarely followed his plans. He didn't get to saddle up until May.

An Internal Hornet's Nest

---

[72] Upham, p. 35.

Washington's Savior

What John Glover ran into in early 1779 was a buzzing hornet's nest of stinging personal matters at the highest levels of the Continental Army. Washington had been making plans to send several divisions of the army into the Wyoming Valley of Pennsylvania to attack and destroy the Indian settlements and villages whose chiefs and warriors had allied themselves with the British and who had been raiding villages and murdering American pioneers on the frontier. Washington was going to take personal command of the entire campaign, but he had two other major generals in mind to command the two divisions of Continental soldiers going on the expedition. They were both trusted by Washington and they both possessed strong anti-Indian reputations.

James Clinton, scion of the great New York gubernatorial family, was already a general already serving with Washington's main army in the New York. The second general was none other than Glover's boss; John Sullivan and he wasted no time in joining Washington and leaving his good friend John Glover in charge until a new commander was named.

The furlough was delayed until the arrival of the new officer. A few days later, Sullivan's replacement rode into camp and it was none other than General Horatio Gates. That did not spell instant relief for Glover, however. Granny was reluctant to let him go and requested he wait until John Stark arrived with additional troops. Even with Stark in camp, Granny tried to keep

Washington's Savior

the Marblehead man in Rhode Island, asking him to complete many small, meaningless tasks. Finally, Glover had had enough delay, even from Granny. He told Gates he could wait no longer, and, by June 1st, he was back in Marblehead.

Although he was glad to be home and he got much of his personal and business work done, he was unable to get free from projects for his superior, Granny Gates. He was spending several days a week in Boston on what felt was army busywork. When he got word that his brigade was going to march back to the New York highlands, he decided to go with them. Brigade records show the unit left Providence on July 7th, with Glover mounted and at the head of the column.

Shortly after they left Providence, a courier caught up with Glover with a message from Washington. It concerned a force of Red Coats that two days earlier had begun raiding isolated Patriot villages along Long Island Sound.

Washington thought the two forces were on a collision course and he wanted Glover to bag them on the morning. Glover felt it was a futile effort but he nonetheless pressed his men to a double-quick march that missed the raiders by a wide margin. Glover and his men reunited with the Continental Army on July 21st.

Chapter 22

The Great Treason

John Glover always seemed to be in the right place at the right time in order to take part in some of the extraordinarily historic or significant events of the American Revolution.

Glover's war record certainly was exemplary and comprehensive. His battle ribbons included Boston, Brooklyn, Kip's Bay, Harlem Heights, Pell's Point, White Plains, Trenton, Saratoga, West Point, Green Brook, Rhode Island and others. There is no doubt he richly deserved the promotion to brigadier general he received in early 1777.

George Washington, while never closely befriending him, seemed to trust him and the commander-in-chief never hesitated to call upon him when the going got tough.

They were, however, two men going in different directions. Washington, of course, had started off at the very top of the army organization chart, and he would and continue to serve until he became his country's living myth, his word being like the utterances of god.

He had so much at stake, however -- his life, liberty and vast property in Virginia would certainly be forfeit if the army lost. His future depended on victory; and he would do almost anything at this point to keep the army, the war and the Revolution intact.

John Glover was different.

As a Congregationalist, freeman, New England seafarer, he always would be different. He could never be part of Washington's circle of Virginia tobacco planting, slave-owning Anglicans friends and acquaintances with very different dreams and desires.

He did not have as much at stake as did Washington. Glover could fight the war and still go home unmolested – too small a fish to fry. He knew it and they did too. He was flinty, sharp, prejudiced and opinionated – and he was never, ever wrong about anything. He would not have had it any other way.

In the fall of 1780, Washington had another chance to involve Glover in another historic event. This was one of the most painful shocks to ever strike the United States Army – the betrayal and treason of Benedict Arnold. Clouds of scandal and controversy had swirled around Arnold ever since he rode into the rebel camp in Cambridge back in 1775. He was always a fighting leader – the British feared him more than any other – but he had troubles off the battlefield with his accounts and his poor and antagonistic relationships with superiors.

Washington did everything he could to try to save him, but it still was not enough. He understood the value Arnold gave the Army as a fighting officer. But after the slights by Gates at Saratoga, he received a Congress-ordered reprimand from Washington on corruption – championed by Joseph Reed, now the war governor of Pennsylvania – a long-time opponent of Arnold. By mid-1779, the General was fed up with it all and he determined to turn his coat.

During his military governorship of Philadelphia, he had acquired a new home partner, his new wife. She was Peggy Shippen, the 19-year-old daughter of a Philadelphia loyalist. In some ways, she was his biggest supporter; she introduced him to British Major John Andre, General Clinton's chief of intelligence and one of her former suitors. It took a long time to strike a deal with the British and it put both men in a position that kept them edge.

To finalize the 16-month negotiation – obviously this was no spur of the moment decision made by the disgruntled general – the pair met ·on September 23rd, 1780, behind the American lines. Under the final agreement reached, Arnold would become a brigadier in the British army; in return, he would surrender the fort at West Point and, if possible, also snap up George Washington. The pair headed back toward West Point – keeping together for the most part, successfully avoiding pickets and sentries.

Three Militiamen

It was about 9 a.m. and Andre had finally separated himself from Arnold. The major was almost to safety when suddenly three men stepped out of a copse of trees to stop the solitary traveler. The morning roads were full of men going to and fro between picket lines, taverns and bivouacs. Andre ran into a wandering trio of militia – John Paulding, Isaac Van Warten and David Williams – all local men more interested in a day of larceny and perhaps murder rather than wandering around in the woods for no godly reason. As soon as they saw Andre, the militiamen moved quickly to catch the well-dressed traveler before he got away,

They wasted little time in stripping him and finding his wallet, which was full of money. Then they found the papers and the pass signed by Arnold himself. They knew they had found something important.

They kept looking at Andre and smiling at him while they discussed the situation. Andre tried to bribe the trio with a watch to no avail; the three had smelled a rat and turned him over to a guard sergeant.

They were Patriots after all.

The news about Arnold spread like wildfire. The turncoat himself fled his home within hours to safety on a British frigate anchored in the Hudson. Washington was on an inspection tour and he arrived at the General's home before Peggy Arnold could escape. According to witnesses who had accompanied the commander-in-chief, she put on a half-clad, Oscar-winning performance that convinced Washington of her innocence. She later joined her husband in British territory.

Washington was shaken to the core – no one event ever shocked him more during the war than Arnold's treachery. He wanted to punish the renegade, but Arnold was safe in New York and Sir Henry Clinton refused to give up his new brigadier. According to military law at the time, Washington would have been well within his rights to bring up charges of spying against John Andre and the British major face a court-martial – basically the same treatment received by Nathan Hale in New York when he was hung back in 1776.

He decided, instead, to hold a full-fledged military tribunal for Major Andre where his guilt or innocence would be decided by 15 of the top soldiers in the Continental Army. Board members included Major General Nathanael Greene, who once again would serve the needs of his commander and his hero by handling the crucial role of chairman of the jury. Judge advocate John Laurence was assigned to gather the evidence and handle the case against the unfortunate Major Andre as chief prosecutor.

Five other major generals served on the Andre panel. They were the Marquis de Lafayette, Robert Howe, Arthur St. Clair, Baron von Steuben, and William Alexander of New Jersey, also known as Lord Stirling.

Giving the court even more authority was the fact that the eight other seats went to top brigadiers in the army. Washington wanted no loopholes, no second-guessing, and no questions. The brigadiers were James Clinton, Edward Hand, Jedidiah Huntington, John Patterson, Henry Knox, Samuel Parsons, curmudgeonly, independent John Stark from New Hampshire, and John Glover.

Since July, John Glover had been away from his brigade on assignment in Springfield,

Mass. where he was in charge of receiving and training all new recruits coming to join the regiments and brigades of the Massachusetts Continental line.

On September 26th, he was already back at the army camp at West Point, having been recalled by Washington to serve on the panel two days earlier. Sitting in his tent that evening, he wrote yet another letter home to his family in Marblehead and outlined to them – the basics of what he called 'Arnold's infernal plot.'

He told them Arnold had gone over to the enemy and now wore the scarlet jacket of a British brigadier in New York, where they say he was itching to lead the king's army against the rebels, his former friends. Glover also was surprised by Arnold's arrogance when he realized West Point was part of the deal, and that Washington's near capture was not accidental.

Three days later, the trial of John Andre began.

The Spy Trial

It was Friday morning September 25th, 1780 and the entire sprawling camp of the Continental Army at West Point seemed to be alive and moving. Since his arrival, John Glover had discovered an interesting fact that surprised him – no one was anxious to see Andre hang. He was apparently a kind, solicitous and polite man who did not have an enemy anywhere. They would have strung Arnold up without a second thought; but probably most of the soldiers would have helped Andre escape.

In reality, Washington felt much the same way. He had no real desire to hang anyone except Benedict Arnold. To that end, he had sent messages and emissaries to talk to General Sir Henry Clinton – who had taken over from General Howe after that worthy had abandoned Philadelphia and asked to be relieved – to seek a trade.

It would be a one-for-one trade, Andre for Arnold, no more, no less. Clinton refused.

The trial would go on.

They all convened that morning at the old Dutch Reformed Church in Tarrytown, in what would later become 'Sleepy Hollow country' when Washington Irving began to write his stories about the region. But this day, General Nathanael Greene presided over the life and death trial of the young Englishman accused of being a spy. George Washington was nowhere to be found.

Earlier, Andre had written a letter to Washington in which he admitted his true identity as General Clinton's chief of intelligence and insisted he simply was doing his job that night. He also said that Arnold had forced him to change out of his uniform. He felt he had acted honorably. That letter now became evidence against Andre.

Prosecutor Laurence then made the case against John Andre, insisting that no matter what he thought, the fact was he was caught behind the lines in civilian clothes.

According to law, that made him a spy.

Greene then asked the board if they had questions. Only Baron von Steuben – himself an enormous fraud – had a few.

The rest were silent.

The board caucused in private. When they were finished, Greene announced the board had unanimously found Major John Andre guilty of spying. The sentence would be carried out tomorrow, Saturday, October 1st, at 5 p.m. Then the court adjourned, only Greene and von Steuben having said a word during the proceedings.

Washington signed the death warrant and other papers needed to finalize the execution. He also told Glover to plan on being officer of the day until the execution was over.

Saturday dawned with a flurry of communication between the lines as General Clinton made a last ditch effort to arrange a trade to save Andre's life. Washington, who was still outraged and livid at what Arnold had attempted, now wanted him back in his hands more than ever. He postponed the hanging by one day and then dispatched General Greene to parlay with the British.

Meeting the enemy without fanfare, Greene presented his proposal quickly – Andre for Arnold was the only trade Washington would make. It was the only trade that the Americans would make and the only one the British couldn't.

Major Andre's fate was sealed.

The Wrong Man Died

Washington's Savior

The crowd gathered quietly on the ground near the fort on October 2nd. General John Glover was Washington's handpicked officer of the day and that meant he was in charge of what was happening at the post that day.

There had been no time to build a gallows; instead, Andre would stand on a wagon, the noose would go around his neck, the horse would move forward and Andre would swing.

Shortly before 5 p.m., muffled drums were heard in the distance; soon the prisoner and his guard approached the execution site. A grave had been dug and a wooden coffin lay nearby.

Andre winced visibly when he saw the wagon and noose and he realized how he would die. He felt he had been promised soldier's death by firing squad. He protested to no avail; he was told that he would receive the sentence that fit his crime.

Glover motioned to the hangman who then assisted Andre in mounting the wagon. Once he was in position, Andre whispered something to his executioner, probably the ritual forgiveness they request before doing their job.

Now the death sentence was read aloud by Colonel Alexander Scammell of Washington's staff, who asked if Andre had any last words. Andre shook his head. Some close to him swore he also said to tell all who ask, that he died like a gentleman. He spoke no more.

The hangman then handed Andre a blindfold, which the British major wrapped around his own head. Then the executioner placed a black silk bag over his head, tied his hands behind his back and moved away. He looked back at General Glover, who was mounted next to Scammell. Glover then raised his arm as a signal to proceed.

The hangman got down from the wagon.

He slapped the horse.

The wagon moved.

John Andre died.

There were no cheers after the body was cut down. Andre was buried quickly, and, at his own request, without benefit of clergy. Most of the Continental Army believed the wrong man was buried that cool October afternoon.

John Andre rested in peace in his 'Sleepy Hollow' grave for 40 years. In 1820, at the request of the Duke of York, his body was exhumed and taken to London. Today, amid the dusty remains of kings and queens, princes and generals, poets and scientists, he sleeps in Westminster Abbey.

Benedict Arnold – his name today is a synonym of treason – eventually led two expeditions against the revolution. In December 1780, he led 1,600 men up the James River and captured the capital city of Richmond and almost bagged the state's war governor, Thomas Jefferson. Arnold's last command, in October 1781, was the taking of Fort Griswold in New London, Conn., not far from his boyhood home in Norwich. In 1810, he died in London, sick, penniless, yet still with his wife Peggy. He was 61.

Washington's Savior

Chapter 23

"The World Turned Upside Down"

After the trial, Glover spent the rest of 1780 and almost all of 1781 with his brigade at a number of the Hudson Highland forts.

He had shown Washington that he was a competent engineer and that he could keep large groups of soldiers busy doing things many other fighting men might have refused to do. Most of Washington's army had not fought since Monmouth, and the soldiers had found siege duty tremendously tedious. The work Glover found for them was hard and dirty, but it did keep the men busy.

His administrative talents, however, may have caused him to miss one of the truly joyous moments of the American Revolution. In the late summer of 1781, almost all of Washington's army began to move out of their lines and earth works and marched south. The French Navy again was coming to the rescue from New York.

They spent a few months making sure Clinton sent no reinforcements to Cornwallis starving on York River. Clinton did eventually send a small flotilla loaded with provisions and men to aid his subordinate, but it arrived too late.

Washington's Savior

Both officers and men from the Continental Army later said they had never seen the General so excited and animated than during the Yorktown campaign. He was jumping from battery to battery, sighting the guns himself, and he actually fired the first shot on October 7th, 1781, letting Cornwallis know that the jig was up.

The British lord expected aid and assistance from Clinton in New York with his 10,000 men, but he watched for British sail in vain. He was trapped and cutoff and he knew it.

As the siege drew to its expected outcome, Washington realized he still had two gifts of heroism left to give out. Whoever he assigned the taking of Redoubts Nine and Ten would surely be applauded by Congress, by the war committee and by the commander-in-chief. So he assigned two of his favorite field commanders to make the attack after dark on October 17th. Major General the Marquis de Lafayette and Lt. Colonel Alexander Hamilton did their jobs well. Cornwallis's last line of defense was gone.

The Lord Looks for Terms

Cornwallis knew it was over and finally he sent word to Washington that he would be willing to discuss the terms of surrender. This was one of the few times during the war that Washington was in a position to grant terms, but he declined. He told Cornwallis all he would accept would be unconditional surrender, done in two days.

At noon on October 19th, all was ready. The British army band played an appropriately sad and melancholy tune. It was not, however, *"The World Turned Upside Down"* – unfortunately, because that would have been perfect because that was what had just happened.

Cornwallis, however, was nowhere to be seen. The aristocratic general could not stand the thought of surrendering to such a gaggle of rabble and he determined not to do so personally. He had feign illness and sent his deputy, Brigadier General Charles O'Hara, to surrender in his place. He insisted O'Hara give the sword to Rochambeau; he must spurn and embarrass Washington if at all possible.

When both armies were in position, O'Hara approached the cluster of American officers, who received him politely. But when he tried to give the sword to Rochambeau, the Frenchman demurred and motioned to Washington as the proper recipient. To the surprise of everyone, he too refused.

Washington reminded O'Hara that in 1780, when Sir Henry Clinton captured Charleston, South Carolina, he had totally humiliated the American commanding general by not allowing him to surrender with honor. Regimental colors were furled, the band was silenced and the military tradition was shattered for the general, who was Glover's compatriot and Washington's old friend, Benjamin Lincoln. Now that Lincoln was Washington's deputy, O'Hara, as Cornwallis's second, was welcome to surrender to the Massachusetts man, to help restore his reputation and end this drama in Virginia.

The stout Irish general was tired and he would play diplomat no longer. He offered his sword to General Lincoln, who took it and then returned it. With that simple, yet reflective gesture, the surrender was done, over, finished.

As Lafayette wrote to a friend on October 22nd, "The play, sir, is over."

Finis

As soon as Washington was certain of victory, he had dispatched a trusted aide, Captain Tench Tilghman, to bring this great news to an anxious Congress waiting to the north in Philadelphia. As he and his mount thundered across the autumn countryside, he shouted to all who could hear that Cornwallis had surrendered. Church bells pealed and bonfires glowed behind him as he made his way north.

Tilghman arrived in Philadelphia on October 24th, and his news set off an extensive and joyous series of picnics, public parties, barbecues and other entertainments that spread like wildfire as many people celebrated with gunpowder what they felt was surely the end of the war.

Within days, the incredible news also reached the Hudson Highlands and the anxious remnants of the Continental Army waiting for Washington's return. They troops exploded with joy when they heard the news.

To commemorate the victory, General Heath

held a day-long picnic for the army which featured special food for the officers and an extra ration of grog for the men. Many of the regiments and other units used freshly cut hay and straw to build effigies of the traitor Benedict Arnold, which they burned when they needed warmth or light.

Across the Sea

It took five weeks for the news about Yorktown to reach London and Lord North. North was King George III's friend, compatriot, companion, chief strategist for North America, his secretary and the king's Prime Minister in the Parliament.

North was a veteran politician and long-time bureaucrat who knew defeat when he saw it and he saw it in that dispatch about Yorktown.

Lord George Germain was with North when the news about Yorktown arrived from Virginia. He later recalled that when North read the report, he was speechless for about half an hour and then he just wandered around mumbling, "oh god, it is finally over."

North was correct. His government was able to survive several more shaky months in power, but the general population – who had never really favored fighting their own colonials – were clamoring for a change.

Lord North finally lost a vote of confidence in Parliament in March of 1782 and his government fell. He was replaced by William Pitt the Younger and his Whig Party. They made sure the Americans got their freedom.

Washington's Savior

The provisional articles of the peace treaty were signed by the commissioners on November 30th, 1782 in Paris. The final treaty of peace between Great Britain and her former thirteen colonies – now known as the United States of America – was signed on September 3rd, 1783.

The impossible had become reality.

Chapter 24

Taps

It was ironic, but John Glover was one of the last of the principles involved to know exactly when his retirement from the Continental Army took place.

The actual date was July 22nd, 1782, less than nine months after Yorktown, and more than a year before Washington's famous farewell to his officers at Fraunce's Tavern in New York in early December of 1783. But it was on July 22nd of 1782 that Congress agreed with Washington and retired John Glover as a brigadier general at half pay. He was 50 years old.

In communicating this to Glover, General Washington wrote on July 30th, 1782, that "I take this earliest opportunity to communicate it for your information. Sincerely wishing you a restoration of your health, attended with every happiness in your future walks of life."

They would meet again.

Glover wondered a bit why this bid to retire was accepted by Washington while other attempts had not passed muster. He had included extensive medical information from his local physician and it must have convinced the General that he was really sick.

What ailed Glover anyway? No one ever

knew for sure, but whatever it was, with Glover it manifested itself as untreatable, unshakable insomnia. This may seem like a minor illness, but a lack of good rest can be debilitating over a long period of time, such as an eight-year revolution.

Glover claimed the sickness had first afflicted him at Saratoga. For nearly five years, he claimed he could sleep no more than two hours at a time, and never more than two nights in a row. He could no longer go on as things were. He wrote to Washington that if he were to inherit a fairy tale kingdom, he could neither walk one mile to claim it nor even ride five miles just to see it.

He could go no longer, and Washington agreed. Both men knew the fighting was over and the Americans knew Benjamin Franklin and John Adams were in Paris negotiating a treaty of peace between Great Britain and the fledgling United States. Washington now knew that Glover was expendable.

Not a Quiet Retirement

Once he was retired and back in Marblehead and safe in the bosom of his family, John Glover had two major objectives for his retirement – to regain and restore his health and his wealth.

As it turned out, the health restoration proved to be the easier of the two tasks to complete. And much of the credit had to go to the new Mrs. Glover. On March 1st, 1781, he had married a woman from Boston, a widow named Frances Hichborn Fosdick. She was a cousin of Paul Revere.

She also may have been related to the Thomas Fosdick who served with Glover in several positions and who sailed one of the fire ships against British frigates in the Hudson River in 1776.

While he was in Providence, Glover had courted several Rhode Island women, but nothing ever came of those relationships.

The new Mrs. Glover took charge of her new husband's family life when he arrived at home to stay. She allowed him long hours of uninterrupted sleep and rest in warm and dry rooms; she made sure he had warm clothes and, she kept him away from business problems for as long as she could. She used the bounty of the sea to create pot after pot of thick, rich, delicious versions of the soups and chowders of the region.

The retired general soon discovered that wealth restoration was going to take a lot longer than expected. We have already seen what the war had done to the town and to its people. Like many other men of similar economic positions, war had depleted most of the Glover assets; apparently even the *Hannah* was gone. People had to be creative. One story has Glover coming home and setting up his cobbler's bench to make shoes to support his family. Quaint as this seems, don't believe it because it never happened. John Glover had sworn to himself years before that he would never again make shoes, and this was one vow he would keep.

Washington's Savior

It took the Marblehead economy a long time to recover from the war. But when the town was ready to rejoin the trading world in the mid-1780s – John Glover was ready too. He was able to obtain loans so he could buy cargoes and lease the ships he needed to trade. The business, however was not consistent, and it fluctuated almost annually, causing the Glovers to have good years and then bad ones.

Such years embittered John Glover as he grew older. The major problem was the impact the off years had on his property taxes. Because he was property-rich, he had substantial annual tax bills that had to be covered even if his trading business was not doing so well. Several times he had to stand by and watch the town auction off parcels of his land to pay the Marblehead levy.

In spite of this, Glover continued to buy land outside of his home district, concentrating on the remote Province of Maine and it the oft-disputed territory called Vermont. In fact, the town of Glover, Vermont, is named for him.

Back Pay

Like other officers of the Continental Army, Glover kept in touch with many of his former comrades. His reasons were mainly financial. The general had not been paid since 1780 and he estimated that he was owed nearly $2,500 in back pay and expenses. It was money he could use to support his family today and it was certainly owed him. He began a lengthy correspondence with the Congress' moneyman Robert Morris from New Jersey. He was sympathetic to Glover, but he was already robbing Peter to pay Paul and a retired general was not that high on the priority list. It does appear, however, that Glover eventually received his back pay.

Glover also wrote a number of letters to Benjamin Lincoln, with whom he served at Saratoga. He may have sought a government position from his fellow Massachusetts general, but nothing was forthcoming.

Glover retained his personal popularity and continued in public service for Marblehead. He was elected a delegate to the Massachusetts constitutional convention, which approved the federal Constitution. Glover also served two terms in the General Court, the state legislature. He spent many years on the town's board of selectmen, and in 1789, as the board's chairman, he was host to none other than the visiting President of the United States – George Washington.

Collector for Marblehead?

Later, when Washington was in his second term, Glover made an attempt to obtain a federal appointment as collector of revenues for the port of Marblehead. In this effort, he was told to work through his old compatriot and current secretary of war, Henry Knox.

He provided Knox with plenty of

information about why he wanted and needed the position and he reminded Knox just what he had accomplished during his years in the Continental Army.

But his words feel on deaf ears. Glover's relationship with Knox was always complex as Knox rose higher in the army's hierarchy and eventually became the first secretary of war. By the time Glover came looking for a favor, Knox was in no mood to grant it. Neither man had seen eye- to-eye with each other on many issues during the eight years of war, and Knox had never forgotten some of the stinging insults Glover had thrown at him, especially about his weight and girth. It is also true that John Glover had never been a man to play internal politics nor did he ever try kissing up to anyone for anything. That would never be his style.

John Glover never got the collector's job or any other federal position.

A New Family Homestead

During the turmoil over what to do with property that had been abandoned by the Loyalists, Glover had been keeping his eyes on a 189-acre farm along the Marblehead/Salem border. Once it was confiscated by the state under the terms of the Confiscation Act of 1777, Glover was able to purchase it at rock bottom prices in 1780.

There, surrounded by his family that included his own surviving children – he had lost a daughter and one of his younger sons during the post-war period – and a growing brood of grandchildren – John Glover would live out the rest of his life.

On January 30th, 1797, John Glover died. The cause of death was listed as hepatitis. He was 64. Washington died in December 1799.

The day after his death, the following obituary appeared in the local Salem *Gazette*:

DIED – At Marblehead, of a hepatick disease, John Glover. Esq., aged 62 (sic). As a military character he stood high on the list of fame, and acted a very distinguished part in those judicious plans and arrangements which led on to the capture of Burgoyne and his army, and was honored with the superintendency of them in their march through the country as the most qualified person. He was officer of day when Major Andre made his exit; which, though the effect of the necessity, deeply affected the General, and drew tears from every eye. In private life, he was the warm and steady friend...with no dissimilulation. He was the affectionate husband, the kind brother, the best of fathers. Free from every appearance of guile and in civil capacity he sustained some of the first offices within the gift of his fellow citizens and ever conducted to their appreciation. He was chosen a delegate to the state convention for the purpose of assenting to and ratifying the Federal Constitution, and has ever been one of its warmest supporters.

His tombstone reads

Erected with filial respect to
the Hon. John Glover, Esquire
Brigadier General in the
Late Continental Army
Died January 30, 1797

Age 64

Epilogue

Remembrances of a bygone era

During the passage of the years, attempts have been made to re-discover John Glover and to honor his contributions to our fight for independence.

One came quickly.

Shortly after the British finally left the continent, Congress honored a number of people who had lent much of themselves to the 'glorious cause.' They did not forget John Glover. In recognition of his years of service, he was promoted to brevet or temporary Major General. He made no effort to turn this promotion down.

A True Local Hero

Of course, the geography of his native Marblehead is liberally sprinkled with his surname, from Glover Hill to Glover Circle to Glover School.

The Marblehead Historical Society and Museum also collects and displays all things Glover.

On Guard

Washington's Savior

In today's city of Boston, a bronze statue of a dismounted yet well-armed General John Glover has been guarding Commonwealth Avenue for more than a century. The statue itself is entitled *General John Glover, A soldier of the Revolution*.

Glover also was not forgotten four score and seven years after the Revolution during the American Civil War. The town named its Civil War facility **Camp Glover**. There is little doubt which side he would have favored.

Glover's Rock

On October 18th, 1901, the Mount Vernon, New York, chapter of the Daughters of the American Revolution unveiled a special plaque noting the 125th anniversary of the Battle of Pell's Point. It honored 'Glover's Rock,' the huge granite outcropping on which the en of Marblehead anchored their defense that once again saved the Continental Army.

The Rev. O.B Lovejoy of Mt. Vernon, gave the benediction.

The bronze plague is still visible today and on that large rock on the shore of Pelham Bay.

GLOVER'S ROCK

IN MEMORY OF THE 550 PATRIOTS WHO LED BY COL. JOHN GLOVER, HELD GENERAL HOWE'S ARMY IN CHECK AT THE

Washington's Savior
BATTLE OF PELL'S POINT,
OCTOBER 18, 1776, THUS AIDING
WASHINGTON
IN HIS RETREAT TO WHITE PLAINS.

Fame is the perfume of heroic deeds.

The Sanctity of Trenton

The almost religious aura of Trenton continued to grow in reputation to nearly mythic levels during the years after the war when it was always celebrated as key to the ultimate victory.

Years after the famous battle, the Massachusetts state legislature in Boston hosted a special speaker to lecture on that topic. His name was Henry Knox, the former artillery general and the successor to Washington. Now rather long in the tooth, slow in the saddle and clouded in memory, Knox was no longer a Bostonian though he still lived in the state – his estate – Montpelier – was in Thomaston in the district of Maine.

He told the legislators:

I wish this body knew THE people of Marblehead well as I do – I wish that they had stood on the banks of the Delaware River in 1776 on that bitter night when the commander-in-chief had drawn up his little army to cross it, and had seen the powerful current bearing onward toward the floating masses of ice, which threatened destruction to whoever would so venture onto its bosom.

I wish that when this occurrence threatened to the

266

army along the perilous path to the unfading glories
and honors in the defeat the enterprise, they could
have heard that distinguished warrior demand *"who
will lead is on?'* and soon the men of' Marblehead
and Marblehead ALONE, stand forward to lead
achievements of Trenton.

There, sir, went the fishermen of Marblehead, alike
at home on land and water, alike ardent, patriotic
and unflinching while unfurling the flag of
democracy.[73]

These were fine words by a fine man about
a fine military unit, but there was one thing
missing – any mention of their leader Col. John
Glover.

It makes one wonder. Glover was so closely
linked with men from Marblehead that one was
rarely mentioned without the other. Was Knox
simply forgetful or did he continue to object to the
way Glover left the army and Washington in
1782? Did he feel that Glover disrespected the
Virginian and might have done things to injure
his memory?

Did Knox feel that Glover had a better
fighting reputation as line general than he did as
a staff general? Did Knox despise Glover that
much?

We shall never know.

GEO. WASHINGTON SLEPT HERE

But John Glover understood more than

Upham, p. 18.

most the value of service to his community and the rewards it can bring. In the 1780s, Glover was not only working to rebuild his business, but the Town of Marblehead as well. To do that, he served several terms on the board of selectmen (New England's version of a town council) in a variety of positions including that of chairman.

He was serving in that position in 1789 when he was told the President of the United States was going to be touring New England that autumn and he wished to see the port of Marblehead, the god-forsaken home of one of his old school generals. It would require Chairman Glover to welcome President Washington to the town and then escort him through the community.

Both men were dressed in their finest when they met, never probably expecting to see each other again. They both knew the debt they owed each other.

For everything.

Washington arrived in his carriage having made is way up the great Boston Post Road from the capital. No transcript of the meeting has survived; if either man wrote a diary entry, it was either torched by Martha – she burned thousands of Washington's – and Frances, may have done the same with Glover's.

This is my fictional account of their meeting.

The two men, both the same age, walked differently. The President still used his long legs to his advantage, taking long strides. Glover, still short and stocky, had to take more steps to cover the distance.

As the door shut on them, Washington spoke first. "General, it is so good to see you again and to see you in such good health. It has been a long time since we parted, and much has happened to both of us." Glover nodded.

"You much more than me, Your Excellency."

The President laughed. "Our friend Mr. Adams is always thinking up new titles for me to use, but I much prefer General myself."

Glover nodded, noting that General was the title he preferred and he had Washington to thank for that.

Washington shook his head.

"You and your men earned every honor you received; you saved our army and our cause several times. And now, since this is Massachusetts and the state of equality, we are both equal. So you call me George and I will call you John.

"Now, show me this Marblehead I've heard so much about".

Finally

In 1972, a large older home at 11 Glover Street in Marblehead was added to the United States Register of Historic Sites. It was John Glover's homestead, where he and his family lived from the 1750's to 1780, when he moved his clan to the new home he purchased from the state government's inventory of confiscated Loyalist properties. The original Marblehead property is

Washington's Savior

now the John Glover National Historic Site.

Bibliography

ORIGINAL DOCUMENTS

Gen. John Glover Papers and Collection, Massachusetts Historical Society, Boston, Mass.

Upham, William, *A Memoir of General John Glover of Marblehead,* Charles Swasey, Salem, 1863.

Sanborn, Nathan, *General John Glover and his Marblehead regiment in the Revolutionary War,* published by the Marblehead, Mass., Historical Society, 1903.

The George Washington Papers, The Library of Congress, Washington, DC. On-line collection.

The George Washington Papers, the University of Virginia, Charlottesville, Va., On -line collection.

BOOKS

Anderson, Fred, *The Crucible of War,* Vintage, New York, 2000.

Billias, George Athan, *General John Glover and his Marblehead Mariners.* Holt Rinehart and Winston, New York, 1960.

Billias, George Athan, editor, *George Washington's Generals and Opponents,* Da Capo

Press, New York, 1994.

Brayall, Richard, *"To The Uttermost of My Power"* – *The Life and* Times of Sir *William Pepperrell. 1696-1759,* Heritage Books, Westminster, MD.,2008.

Bobrick, Benson, *Angel in the Whirlwind,* Penguin Books, New York, 1997.

Bourneman, Walter, *The French and Indian War: Deciding the Fate of North America,* HarperCollins, New York, 2006.

Brands, H.L., *The First American,* Vintage, New York, 2003.

Browning, Reed, *The War of The Austrian Succession,* St. Martin's New York, 1998.

Buchanan, John, *The Road to Guilford Courthouse,* John Wiley & Son, New York, 1997.

Carter, Jimmy, *The Hornet's Nest,* Simon & Schuster, New York. 2003.

Cook, Fred, *The Golden Book of the American Revolution,* The Golden Press, New York, 1959.

Colonial Society of Massachusetts, *Publications of the Colonial Society of Massachusetts,* Boston, 1900.

Cuneo, John, *Robert Rogers of the Rangers,* Fort

Ticonderoga Museum, Ticonderoga, N.Y, 1958.

Eisenhower, John S.D., Editor, *Battles* of the *Revolutionary War*, Da Capo Press, 1992.

Fast, Howard, *The Crossing*, iBooks, New York, 1971.

Fleming, Thomas, *Liberty*, Viking, New York, 2001.

Flexner, James Thomas, *Washington: The Indispensable Man*, Little Brown, Boston, 1974. .

Fischer, David Hackett, *Washington's Crossing*, Oxford University Press, New York, 2004.

Gallagher, John J. *The Battle of Brooklyn*, 1776, Sarpedon Books, New York, 1997.

Golway, Terry, *Washington's General*, Henry Holt, New York, 2005..

Hatch, Robert McConnell, *Major John Andre*, Houghton Mifflin, Boston, 1986.

Hibbert, Christopher, *George* III, Basic Books, New York, 1998.

Hibbert, Christopher, *Redcoats and Rebels*, Avon Books, New York, 1990.

James, Edward, *The Rise and Fall of the British Empire*, Abacus Books, London, 1994.

Ketchum, Richard, *Decisive Day, the Battle for Bunker Hill,* Anchor Books, New York,1974.

Ketchum, Richard, *The Winter Soldiers,* Owl Books, New York, 1999.

Ketchum, Richard, *Saratoga; The Turning Point of America's Revolutionary War,* Henry Holt, New York, 1994.

Ketchum, Richard, *Victory at Yorktown,* Henry Holt, New York, 2006.

Langguth, A.J., *Patriots,* Touchstone Books, New York, 1989

Lengel, Edward, *This Glorious Struggle -- George Washington's Revolutionary War Letters,* Smithsonian Books, New York, 2007.

Leckie, Robert, *A Few Acres of Snow -- The Saga of the French and Indian Wars,* John Wiley And Son, New York, 1999,

Leckie, Robert, *George Washington's War,* Harper New York, 1990.

Leckie, Robert, *The Wars of America,* Harper & Row, New York, 1968.

Lomask, Milton, *Aaron Burr,* Farrar Strauss and Giroux, New York, Vol. 1, 1979; Vol. 2, 1982.

Washington's Savior

Malone, Dumas, *Jefferson the Virginian*, Little Brown, Boston, 1948.

Martin, Joseph Plum, A *Narrative* of A *Revolutionary Soldier*, Signet Classics, New York, 2001.

McCullough, David, *1776*, Simon and Schuster, New York, 2005.

McCullough, David, J*ohn Adams*, Simon and Schuster, New York, 2000.

Miller, Nathan, *Broadsides*, John Wiley and Son, New York, 2000.

Middlekauf, Robert, *The Glorious Cause*, Oxford University Press, New York, 1986.

Nelson, James L. *Benedict Arnold's Navy*, McGraw Hill, New York, 2006.

Parkman, Francis, *Count Frontenac and New France*, The Library of America, New York, 1983.

Parkman, Francis, *A Half Century of Conflict*, The Library of America, New York, 1983.

Parkman, Francis, *Montcalm and Wolfe*, The Library of America, New York, 1983.

Puls, Marc, *Henry Knox*, Palgreve MacMilllian, New York, 2008.

Washington's Savior

Quinn, Arthur, *A New World,* Berkley Books, New York, 1994.

Randall, Willard Sterne, *George Washington,* A *Life,* Owl Books, New York, 1997.

Randall. Willard Sterne, *Benedict Arnold,* William Morrow, New York, 1990.

Roberts, Kenneth, *Arundel,* Doubleday, New York, 1976.

Roberts, Kenneth, *Rabble In Arms,* Doubleday, New York, 1976.

Roberts, Kenneth, *Oliver Wiswell,* Doubleday, 1976.

Roberts, Kenneth, *Northwest Passage,* Ballentine Books, New York, 1991.

Ross, John, *War on the Run,* Bantam, New York, 2009.*tophe 2*

Rose, Ben Z., *John Stark, Maverick General,* Tree Line Press, Waverly, MA. 2007.

Scheer, George F., Hugh H. Rankin, *Rebels and Redcoats.* DaCapo Books, New York, 1987.

Zinn, Howard and Arnove, Anthony, *Voices of A People's History of The United States,* Seven Stones Press, New York, 2004.

Washington's Savior

Ward, Christopher, *The War of the Revolution,* 2 vols. , The MacMillan Company, 1952.

Index

Washington's Savior

50, 54, 55, 57, 58, 73, 76, 81, 82, 87, 174, 180, 183, 186, 188, 214, 220, 221, 222, 224, 230, 240, 268

New Hampshire, xiii, 32, 34, 35, 43, 48, 56, 57, 82, 90, 99, 143, 152, 173, 185, 193, 201, 209, 221, 228

New York, xii, 18, 23, 52, 55, 61, 73, 81, 82, 83, 85, 86, 87, 89, 91, 92, 96, 100, 101, 102, 104, 105, 107, 109, 115, 128, 129, 130, 132, 142, 150, 160, 161, 163, 165, 167, 171, 172, 177, 182, 188, 189, 193, 195, 196, 199, 212, 219, 221, 226, 230, 237, 238, 242, 244, 256, 265, 271, 272, 273, 274, 275, 276

Oriskany, 172, 173, 191

Parliament, 18, 34, 36, 206, 210

Peekskill, 132, 165, 174, 181

Pell's Point, 117, 119, 120, 122, 125, 127, 156, 166, 239, 265

Pepperrell, 21

Philadelphia, 38, 46, 49, 50, 53, 66, 82, 88, 144, 146, 147, 150, 167, 168, 180, 182, 203, 205, 211, 212, 216, 241, 245

Philip Schuyler, 52, 182

Portsmouth, 34, 35, 65, 209

Richard "Black Dick" Howe, 18

Richard Gridley., 60

Samuel Tucker, 71

Saratoga, xii, xiii, 52, 59, 75, 95, 114, 115, 163, 177, 185, 187, 191, 192, 197, 199, 200, 203, 204, 205, 206, 208, 213, 217, 220, 239, 240, 257, 260,

274

Second Continental Congress, 46, 83, 170

Seth Warner, 173

Seven Years War, 20, 189

Sons of Liberty, 39

Stamp Act of 1765., 34

Tallmadge, 105

Thaddeus Kosciusko, 187, 220

the Baron de Residel., 206

the French, 18, 21, 29, 30, 34, 35, 43, 50, 51, 52, 54, 61, 91, 114, 138, 173, 178, 206, 221, 223, 224, 225, 226, 227, 274

the Jamaica Pass, 97, 98

The Salem Alarm, 40, 41

The Turtle, 92

Thomas Jefferson., 39, 85, 248

Throg' s Neck, 120

Ticonderoga, 18, 20, 60, 61, 62, 74, 76, 132, 142, 160, 171, 172, 173, 186, 191, 273

Timothy Pickering, 181

Trenton, xi, xii, 130, 144, 146, 149, 150, 151, 152, 154, 155, 163, 208, 220, 233, 239, 266, 267

Valcour Island, 74

Valley Forge, 60, 203, 211, 212, 213, 214, 217, 218

Virginia, xi, xii, 51, 53, 54, 59, 81, 82, 83, 142, 147, 176, 211, 218, 239, 240, 271

Washington, xi, xii, xiii, 19, 20, 21, 22, 23, 24, 51, 52, 53, 54, 56, 57, 58, 59, 60, 61, 62, 64, 65, 66, 67, 68, 69, 70, 71, 72, 73, 76, 77, 78, 79, 80, 81, 82, 85, 86, 87, 88, 90, 91, 93, 95, 96, 99, 100, 101, 102,

ABOUT THE AUTHOR

RICHARD A. BRAYALL started his career as a newspaper reporter and editor in Lewiston, Maine, before spending the next two decades in public relations for the original AT&T and Ericsson of Sweden.

A graduate of Bates College in Maine and Simmons College in Boston, he lives in New Hampshire with his wife Danita, and close to his three grown sons.

This is his second book.

9 780788 454066